**Douglas Bartles-Smith
and David Gerrard**

Urban
Ghetto

Lutterworth Press

GUILDFORD & LONDON

First published 1976

ISBN 0 7188 2293 5

Printed in Great Britain by
Ebenezer Baylis & Son Ltd.
The Trinity Press, Worcester, and London

Contents

Preface

by David Sheppard, Bishop of Liverpool

Clergymen have an outstanding vantage point to observe what goes on in the inner-city. They are often the only professional people to live there. They are independent of a lot of the sectional interests which colour the views of many. Douglas Bartles-Smith and David Gerrard recognize the strength of the position they are in: it's a refreshing change from the defensive attitude which sometimes only underlines the confusion which some clergymen feel about what their task is.

I saw and respected their work at first hand during the six years when I was Bishop of Woolwich. The twin objectives of this book have been the twin objectives of their ministry: first the proclamation of Jesus Christ and the building up of a locally rooted church: secondly determination to change and remove the limiting and destructive influences of the inner-city.

They have sharp criticisms to offer. As a bishop I have sometimes been the object of that criticism. It has generally been well aimed, and I've been aware that it has come from men who care deeply about people on whose behalf they protest, and who do not write off those whom they criticize.

Government Departments, in setting up the Community Development Project, for example, generally assumed that the answer to inner-city problems could be found within its boundaries. This book adds to the weight of the evidence that this is not true. There are scarce resources in our nation and the inner-city needs to be much more decisively a priority area. Those who want to be persuaded that all is basically well with the way our society is ordered will find no comfort here. The inner-city did not create its own problems. In our society just as it is the same people who are often winners in housing, schools, jobs and facilities, so it is the same people who are losers. We can't expect those who are losers to lose gracefully. This book should help those who are anxious about vandalism or apathy to see that these are generally by-products of a sense of powerlessness and worthlessness. It should also challenge those who care about the task of commending the Christian gospel in the inner-city to see that those who live there will only start to take our proclamation of Christ seriously when they see that we stand for justice even when that is against our own interests.

Introduction

There is no explicit theology in this book, no statements about our religious beliefs. We do not wish the book to be categorized under the label 'Religion' and sold only in church bookshops. We hope it will be read by all those who care about the manifold problems of the inner-city ghettos of our country. We hope they will include clergy and churchwardens as well as journalists and teachers, planners and community workers, dockers and electricians. We would be less than honest, however, if we did not state our belief that the church as an institution is in an excellent position to provide hope and vision for the future of the inner-city. We would also be less than honest if we did not admit that our work and residence in the inner-city, and our writing of this book spring from our Christian commitment. It is because of our belief that God cares for the poor and the powerless that we do not think that the church can exist as a holy huddle, as a pietistic refuge from a torn and changing world. The central core of Jesus' teaching was about the kingdom of God, and he did not shrink from harshly criticizing those who oppressed and persecuted and ignored the poor. This book is an attempt to describe what needs to be done to transform the urban ghettos in our society. It is also an implicit attempt to apply the theology of the kingdom of God to the inner-cities of our country.

1. The Inner-City

The city has been seen for centuries as the centre of learning, artistic endeavour and human community. Today it is difficult to view cities as anything but the abscesses of a malignant global disease, a symptom of the cancerous ills of industrial society.

The festering slums which lie at the decaying heart of all old cities constitute one of the most serious social and political problems in the world today. In the past two hundred years thousands of millions of people have poured from the countryside into the cities. The problems of poverty, bad housing, racialism, crime, alcoholism, physical illness and mental breakdown all exist in their most acute forms in city slums. The continuing flight from the land sustains and exacerbates the urban crisis.

London was the first city to experience the process of assimilating immigrants from the countryside and incorporating them into a huge new urban structure. Other cities have followed a parallel pattern. The problems of London prevail in most other cities. The attempted solutions are similar. Before these can be examined, it is essential to examine the conditions which exist in the inner-city, to see how these have developed, and to describe the culture of the city-dwellers. Nothing is preventing the transformations that are needed in the cities more than the erroneous belief that the situation in the cities is known and catalogued. It is impossible to apprehend the city from the outside. Most accounts of urban problems have been written by people who do not live in the situation which they are describing. This crippling distortion has warped their viewpoints and prevented the radical reappraisal which is a necessary preliminary to widespread action.

The distortion is also a handicap to the organizations which have attempted to ameliorate or reform the conditions in the inner-city. Without immersion in the inner-city it is possible neither to discover the resources available nor to discern the many barriers to reclamation. Many have offered external aid to remedy the deprivation in the inner-city. This has not only failed to improve the conditions, but in many instances has also caused further deterioration by creating greater dependency and dissuading people from helping themselves. This is especially true of the comprehensive network of state and local authority services which has offered the myth of universal help and care which it is totally beyond their powers to deliver. The smaller voluntary agencies working closer to the problems have proved more flexible, more humble, more realistic about their aims, and less grandiose in their aspirations. People will only become more self-reliant with some withering away of the monstrous apparatus of statutory care.

If the inner-city is to be radically regenerated it must occur from a combination of external professional help and the corporate endeavours of its inhabitants. This co-operation will never succeed until the professionals live as well as work in the inner-city. They must learn to work with and not just give aid to the people they profess to serve. There is no other way that the apathy, cynicism and fatalism of the city-dwellers can be overcome, and the invisible walls that surround the urban ghetto can be destroyed.

All cities are different. Yet their very disparity conceals many similarities. The size of the urban mass, the numbers of inhabitants involved, the diversity of their backgrounds, jobs, homes, education, the complexity of city services, and the economic factors which affect the cities' growth and decline are diverse. Yet when we deal with the disadvantages of citizens living clustered together near the core of the city certain common patterns emerge.

Housing

The first and most basic is housing. The external appearance of homes and the interior condition and amenities reflect the social standing of the inhabitants both of individual homes and of whole areas. Inadequate accommodation destroys the lives of families. Dirt and damp, noise and rats and smells can sap the energy and destroy the hopes of those who must endure them.

The squalid conditions of so much housing at the centre of so many cities in Britain, Europe, America and throughout the world should need no emphasis. Few subjects in this country have been the centre of so many government reports, the language and descriptions of which echo each other eerily down the decades. There is still an unacceptably large number of grossly sub-standard housing in the inner-city which should have been renovated or destroyed many years ago. In London one quarter of the families share a home. Half of them have also to share bathrooms. One in eight have to share cooking or washing facilities. A quarter have no bathrooms at all, and one in ten live in acutely crowded conditions often with two rooms or less for every three people. 15% of the stock of London's housing is structurally unfit, that is 340,000 homes, while another 200,000 homes are badly in need of repair. Altogether one quarter of the total housing stock is inadequate. One family in four lives in dilapidated conditions with little space, comfort or privacy. These are the average figures for the whole of London. It is far worse in the inner-city areas, where the proportions of old, overpopulated, rented, shared homes lacking hot water, baths and inside toilets far exceed those in the suburbs. In some areas over half the homes are unfit to live in.

It is easy to go on repeating the endless statistics, referring to the housing facts which different local authorities produce, and which government surveys reiterate, yet the welter of figures cannot achieve the poignancy of individual knowledge. It is a surprise, however great the prominence given to housing statistics, to know that in the 1970's century-old tenements still existed lit only by gas, with communal cold-taps as the only source of running water, and six hall-toilets shared by fourteen families. It is shocking that roofs leak, fungoid walls are wringing wet, and families keep dogs to kill the rats. Old people have to go out of their back door to the yard-toilets in the winter nights through rain and sleet. Homes are so lacking in fire-protection that they are like bonfires awaiting

3

one spark to be destroyed. Yet millions live like this in this country.

This is the condition of the old housing at the centre of so many cities. It is being changed, though not as fast as many would wish. While it is changing, the inhabitants exist in the limbo of redevelopment. The procedures vary from city to city, but there are common features. First comes a rumour that the area is to be destroyed or renovated. Secondly there is a definite hint from the local authority that this is true. Then there are the legal battles, the owners striving for the best possible price, the appeals and counter-appeals. Finally the families leave. Their homes are either destroyed or renovated. The whole process takes from five to ten years. It is difficult to exaggerate the agonies of uncertainty, hope and despair which the residents endure.

As soon as the first rumours start, the owners stop virtually all repairs, maintenance and decoration, regarding them as a wasted investment on doomed properties. Whatever the pleas, threats, legal actions, it is impossible to force the owners to care for the properties. The tenants also tend to stop maintaining the properties. They don't decorate the interiors, they postpone buying new fittings and furniture. In some cases they literally pack all their goods into suitcases and boxes, and camp in their homes, living out of boxes for the next five or ten years. The planning blight, the rapidly deteriorating properties, the leaks, creaks and breaks of old dying homes lead to a rapid disintegration of community morale.

Worst of all is the uncertainty. In some areas council officials and local councillors come year after year saying, 'By next year you will have moved', and return with the same bleak message the following year. Reliable information is impossible to obtain, and the planning procedures are unimaginably tortuous. One poor woman went to her local council's housing offices and asked when she was due to be moved, and was told by the clerk checking her files that her house had already been demolished. 'But I only left it an hour ago,' she said. 'I am sorry,' replied the clerk, 'you must be mistaken; our records clearly show it was pulled down last week.'

As the time for removal finally draws near, the situation gets

4

worse. Councils tend to move out the leaders of the local community, the committee members of tenants' associations first of all. As families move out one by one, the empty homes harbour more rats, dirt and disease. They become worse fire-traps. They are frequently vandalized. The refuse collection deteriorates, and as demolition sometimes begins on empty properties, there is increased noise, dust and dirt.

Finally all the houses are cleared, though some may remain empty for years. Others may be demolished, while the site is left as a deserted wilderness for decades as plans for its future use shift and change.

These are the first two groups of people living in the inner-city: residents living in old, often inadequate accommodation, and those in the process of being redeveloped. Both tend to be composed of predominantly low paid workers, forced by their work and low income to live near to the centre of cities, yet denied access by their poverty to decent living conditions.

Sadly the eventual forced move due to redevelopment does not lead to a radical change in the lives of the rehoused. In some cities they are transferred to bleak housing estates miles from the city centre. They are cut off by poor transport from the amenities of the city. These estates lack shops, halls, clubs and jobs. Manchester and Glasgow are cities with large numbers of such estates. But around most cities, the suburban owner-occupiers dread the intrusion of large municipal housing developments and refuse to release the land to build them. So often the new housing estates are erected on the sites of the old slums. This is frequently in accord with the wishes of their occupiers as they have no wish to move far from their roots. The inner-city with all its faults of noise, dirt, poor amenities and environment also represents strong economic and social ties with general convenience, accessibility and closeness to work.

The poor are displaced from their old slums as a result either of their demolition or of their renovation into desirable habit-ations for the professional middle classes. They move either to similar, if slightly superior old privately rented accommodation, or more usually into council accommodation, the majority of it on huge council estates. For years they have been waiting for rehousing, all their hopes and aspirations focused on the mighty event. They are leaving the old slum for a new life. It is a tremendous event. Young children climb into their new bath and turn on the taps, sitting fully clothed in the rising water. Their parents indulgently thrill to the luxuries of a bath, a kitchen rather than the corner of a room to cook in, a bedroom of their own, decent heating and a front-door key belonging solely to them. None should grudge them such improvements, but before long the grumbles begin to be heard. There are complaints about the high rents, poor amenities, lack of space. There is usually no garden, no play-space. The noise, the vandalism, the distance from schools and shops are deplored.

The truth penetrates. They are far better off than they were, but they are still grossly underprivileged and discriminated against in terms of education, housing, and employment, compared to the middle classes who hold them in low social esteem. They are without power. Due to their shrinking numbers and the increasing complexity of society their chances of rectifying the situation are miniscule.

There have been gigantic difficulties facing local authorities engaged in building homes. They have been facing them since nearly one hundred years ago, when the councils began to replace the Victorian philanthropists who built large blocks of tenements for the workers. Much of the building has been slum clearance rather than rehousing. Architectural styles and fashions have swung bewilderingly fast from High Victorian to neo-Georgian, to concrete slab blocks, to high point blocks, to mixed development, to the demise of tall towers and to medium rise. There has been a shortage of land and of money. There have been frequent political reverses of policy. The Housing Cost Yardstick exercised by the Ministry of Housing has resulted in low quality housing. It has caused the dull uniformity of the housing, the lack of trees and landscaping, the slowness of the lifts, the poor durability. Money has been tight. Interest charges have become prohibitive. The London Borough of Camden's interest payments since 1971 have exceeded the total income from rents by 30 %.

As if this were not enough, the estates were planned by outside professionals who had little knowledge of, or consideration for those who were to live in an environment which they determined. Planners lived in random communities yet planned total communities. Traffic managers whose children played in gardens and not streets planned the new road patterns. Their wives had never been accosted as they walked in underground tunnels under arterial roads to the new shopping developments which replaced the informal bevy of street markets and corner shops to which people were accustomed. Architects never live in anything remotely like the council flats they have designed. Consciously or not, they designed the exact opposite to their own living accommodation. Not houses with gardens, but gardenless flats with tiny bedrooms just big enough for two beds. There is one living room in which the parents have to watch television, the children play records, do homework or entertain friends, and the whole family have to eat. All in 150 square feet. But if the flats seem unlikely to provide adequate living conditions for the next eighty years, the estates as a whole are disastrous.

They are designed as a total environment. They are shut off from their surroundings, isolated compounds, distinctive and distant. Flats are reached by lifts which are slow, crowded, often unworking, fouled by children or dogs. These lifts have to be used not only by residents, but also by postmen, milkmen, or coalmen delivering sacks of coal to eleventh-floor flats heated solely by coal fires. Other flats can only be approached by stairs and concrete walkways for which no one is responsible and from which no one can be prevented access. So dirt, vandalism, and noise are omnipresent. No one is responsible, so few try to prevent abuses. A few difficult families can make life a living nightmare for many others on an estate, yet families with many children often have the most acute social need of rehousing. People grow a carapace of indifference to survive. On the estates, the homes are built first, everything else later. So there are no play areas, no good cheap shops, schooling is often difficult, garages are rare, parking is scarce and many accidents result. There are few areas of natural meeting, nowhere to sit and rest, to stand and talk, or to kiss and hold hands. There is no individuality. There is great isolation but little privacy. The end result of architects designing homes for occupants without their

7

views or ideas or experience is totally unsatisfactory. An architect should know who is his client. The residents have not had the rights of clients. Their wishes and desires, their accumulated experiences have been neither discovered nor interpreted by the architect. The future occupants have never been asked whether they *want* a totally new estate from which all existing historic and familiar landmarks have been obliterated. They have not been consulted about the huge areas in the estates which are neither public nor private space, not designed for play, recreation, gardening or privacy. These spaces are a no-man's-land that police do not patrol, that residents cannot defend nor children play on: a vandal's delight.

Poverty

The second great disadvantage of the inner metropolitan areas is the lack of money of its inhabitants. One of the great myths of suburban life is that not only are the working classes heavily subsidized but they earn huge wages which they squander rather than save. The reality of the situation is quite different. The majority of men in the inner-cities have low paid jobs with little security. Many are employed in public transport, the public utilities, food-processing and service industries (most of which are poorly paid). Many of the workers are unskilled, and those who are skilled tend towards jobs of a practical nature – mending, repairing, decorating. They tend not to be skilled at talking in committees, organizing, co-ordinating, administrating, the parasitical abilities which bring wealth and prestige in society. They are takers of advice and not givers, lacking assurance and confidence in their working lives. In any economic slump they tend to be the workers who are laid off first. In 1975 over 12 % of Stepney's workers were unemployed, compared to a national average of 4% . They have a far higher level of unemployment than usual, especially among the young; and worst of all among the young immigrants unemployment is 10 % higher in Inner London than in South East England. They lack the job security that is the assured and accustomed right of the middle classes. Sick pay at work, time off for family problems and an adequate pension are not the automatic safeguards against misfortune that they are in white-collar jobs. They work longer hours than the national average, have to clock on or sign in for work which tends to be repetitive and boring. They have shorter holidays and less say in when they take them than white-collar workers or managers. All this for considerably less money. Less than one in twenty unskilled workers earns more than the average national wage.

As a result of these low wages and as a result of the depressing housing conditions, more and more women go out to work. Some of the deleterious effects of this on the rearing of children and the weakening of family and community ties will be mentioned later. Women still have an even worse employment deal than their husbands. Part-time jobs and jobs that can be done at home are in short supply and high demand so that they are very poorly paid. Many women slave away at piece work in the home for the clothing industry. Many work in shops. Many go out early in the morning or late in the evenings cleaning schools, offices and public buildings. All these jobs are poorly paid, usually without any security, benefits or pensions.

Inner-city inhabitants are poorly housed and have poorly paid, unrewarding jobs and inadequate family incomes. In some inner-city areas over 90 % of the families are eligible for grants for rent reductions under the Housing Finance Act. Half the tenants of the Greater London Council, the largest municipal housing authority in the world, are eligible for rent rebates. They are also eligible because of their low incomes for a multiplicity of other allowances, rebates and free services. The vast majority of these are means-tested. Less than half the benefits are claimed as a result of the complicated procedures involved. All benefits are liable to be lost with increases of income. This poverty trap discourages employers from raising wages and employees from actively searching for a rise. Workers in the lowest earning brackets, most of whom live in the inner-city, can lose up to 85 % of their wage increases through loss of allowances. As well as the grinding poverty, the psychological effect on a worker of being unable to feed, clothe or house his family without outside help is considerable.

Poor wages means that the worker is condemned to live in poor accommodation. Many are actually still moving into accommodation without bath, hot water or inside toilet, and in poor structural condition. They move because their families have increased and they need more room, or to escape bad landlords, or because they are recently married, or because they have been evicted. Those in such accommodation have no hope (except that of council rehousing) of escape to better homes. Nor do they have the time or money to desert their neighbourhood for short periods. One in four of the middle-income families in the London Borough of Kensington has a second home it can migrate to when it is weary of its congenial area of the inner-city. Nobody in the less salubrious London Borough of Hackney has such a second home.

The Environment

Housing and poverty would be enough of a disadvantage for anyone, but the tragedy of the inner-city is the massive constellation of problems and deprivations which beset its residents. The general environment is a third major problem. There is a huge contrast between the population density in the inner-city and the suburbs. The London Borough of Harrow has 86 people per residential hectare, while Hammersmith has 319 to the hectare; Bromley has 70 people to Tower Hamlets' 333. The high densities in the inner-city areas result in a lack of open space, parks, playgrounds, gardens and woods. They cause grave stress to children and parents. The inner-city areas suffer from excessive traffic. Both cars and large lorries career through residential streets. Commuters park in inner-city areas before catching buses or tubes into central shopping and office areas. The streets, often used as unofficial play areas by children who have nowhere else to play, become death-traps. There is also the noise, dirt, dust, fumes and general inconvenience caused by high traffic volume. Traffic is not a difficulty solely experienced by the inner-city areas, but it is experienced there in a particularly virulent form. The same is true of pollution. It is an international problem. In the inner-city it is worst because of the preponderance of vehicular traffic, of old dangerous factories and old-fashioned mill chimneys and power stations whose emissions poison the surrounding areas. Even the weather is worse in the inner-city than in the suburbs, with considerably less sunshine as a result of the pall of smoke that overhangs industrial areas. Additionally there is the pollution which comes from the sheer density of population, the litter, the broken glass, the dirty city streets, the crumbling buildings, the exterior mould, the animal excreta, the human excreta of the tramps and the vagrants who drift aimlessly in the centre of the cities, the obscenities carved or painted on walls, all the small annoyances which accumulate into a dirty and unpleasant living and working environment.

Housing, poverty, traffic, lack of amenities and lack of space, environmental pollution are all factors in the urban ghetto. Together they have resulted in a whole mass of secondary problems which exacerbate and perpetuate the situation. These are the problems of health, cultural deprivation, education, community disintegration, and the dependent character of the inhabitants of the inner-city which make the situation so complex and so desperate.

Health deprivation begins in the womb. Inner-city mothers are less likely to use efficient methods of birth control, so more unwanted children are conceived and more are born. The mothers seek medical help later during pregnancy than suburban mothers. More babies in the inner-city are born prematurely and under weight. Their standards of hygiene and nutrition are lower than the national average. More inner-city children have serious dental troubles at an earlier age than suburban children. More suffer from cerebral diseases. More are subnormal. Far more children suffer from extreme behavioural problems. As they grow older the health, particularly the mental health of the community continues to be far worse than average. There are four times as many schizophrenics in Tower Hamlets as the national average.

As the inhabitants of the inner-city suffer from bad health so they suffer from poor education. From the late nineteenth century it was always a struggle to persuade, cajole or force children to go to school. The parents needed the children's earning power, and the educational structures have always favoured the middle classes at the expense of the working classes. By creaming off the ablest children into grammar schools and

11

thus to higher education, the deprived areas were dispossessed of the ablest leaders.

The schools in the inner-city are often as old and crumbling as the surrounding housing. As with the housing there are often only outside toilets, damp staircases, leaking roofs and inadequate space for the children to play. There is a very high turnover of young, inexperienced teachers who find it difficult to control children who enter the schools with little discipline. The children lack the confidence to exercise choice without guidance and direction. The levels of attainment in inner-city areas are very poor. There is alienation between the schools and the parents who feel they can contribute nothing to the school or to their children's education. The parents are seldom involved in the schools which remain outposts of middle-class values.

The lack of educational achievements by inner-city children mirrors their environmental background. Nearly a million inner-city children have bad housing conditions, and come from a low income family which has either one parent or more than four children. These are more likely to be law-breakers in care of the local authority, or to have an unemployed father. The average child of a professional family at the age of seven has a reading age four years in advance of a child of unskilled parents. The first seven-year-old has an average reading age of nine, the second of five. The disparity continues and increases with secondary education whether it is selective or comprehensive. At eleven there are 50 % more backward children in Inner London than in England as a whole. One in six cannot read any simple text book and one in two is a backward reader. Only one in twenty has good academic ability. The pressure of neighbourhood and class predominate. There are 103 Local Education Authorities in England and they can be graded according to the Registrar General's classification of professions in social classes one to five. Solihull headed the list with 36 % of its population falling into the social class groupings one and two, those from professional and managerial groups. It also headed the further education rankings with 18·5 % of its schoolchildren getting to university. On the other hand the Borough of Bootle had the lowest class rankings with only 8 % of its population in social groups one and two and 44 % of its population in social groups four and five, those from unskilled and semi-skilled groups. Bootle, unsurprisingly, had the lowest percentage of children reaching university. This discrepancy is as marked for the numbers of children in sixth forms as it is for the numbers of university places, far more Solihull children staying on into the sixth form than Bootle children. Over the country as a whole at least four middle-class children go to university for every working-class child. The picture is even more gloomy when the situation is broken down inside the large Local Education Authority areas. The Inner London Education Authority has under half the national average numbers of its pupils going to further education. That is bad, but it is far worse when it is realized that almost all these children come from areas containing a high proportion of professional families, virtually none of them from the inner-city areas at the central core of the authority. Less than 6 % of the families in North Southwark were in social class two, and none in social class one. In the good and typical local comprehensive school that served the area less than one child in six got one or more 'O' level passes. Out of the whole school with an annual intake of 240 children a year there were only five 'A' Level passes one year. No single child went on to university or any form of higher education.

In the inner-city only a miniscule number of children obtain the opportunities to benefit from higher education. The brighter children are deprived of a good education while the slower and more disadvantaged children opt out of the educational structures completely. All that raising the school leaving age has meant is a longer period of truanting for many children and more strain on the Educational Welfare Service.

Community Decline

Despite the lack of health and the poor education in the inner-city probably the most serious result of the inequalities of wealth, housing and environmental conditions has been the decline of strong viable communities. Although it is false to suppose that all urban slums supported happy and united communities in the nineteenth and early twentieth centuries, the inertia and despair which have always been endemic in areas of urban stress have recently increased. The inhabitants of the urban ghetto have never had adequate housing, decent working conditions or reasonable pay. They have had no share of power, a poor education, authoritarian leadership, and a fixed position at the foot of the social ladder. This has pre-empted any radical change in their situation. They have been materially, culturally and educationally deprived. Fatalism and apathy have resulted. There have been improvements at work. The rise of unions has helped improve wages and conditions. But past indignities and shame of such workers as dockers have resulted in an absolute refusal to trust management, and has contributed to the appalling labour relationships in Britain. The rise of the Labour Party has meant control of local government in many inner-city areas, and a rapid extension of municipal housing, with the council being seen as a much more desirable and responsible landlord than the private owner.

But overall, apathy has predominated and a ghetto mentality has grown. This has intensified as the central city areas have deteriorated. As the Victorian tenements and houses grew older, the middle classes fled the declining area. Transport improvements have continued to encourage them to move further out into the suburbs. The bright and successful members of the working classes have also joined the suburban rush. This has accelerated the decline, leaving the areas tragically short of good indigenous leaders. The result has been that the leaderless communities have suffered most. They have received far more than their share of polluting factories, of new highways driven through the demolished sites of old streets; far less than their share of amenities. Apathy results from powerlessness. The dwellers in the inner-city have vastly less power, wealth, and knowledge to control their destiny than other sections of society. The working classes in the inner-city areas of England and other western countries have very little more chance of improving their conditions, of finding access to the sources of power, than have the blacks in South Africa who have been torn from their homes and relocated in townships. Class is as great a barrier as race. Both stem from ignorance, the ignorance which a privileged and powerful section of the community has of the conditions of an unprivileged and powerless group in the same community. Social justice will not result from abject ignorance.

The decline of a community and its resultant apathy perpetuates a cycle of deprivation which negates the facile optimism of planners and politicians that all one has to do is to provide new houses all round and the problems will disappear. Even if all the inadequate homes in the inner-city could be destroyed or renovated in the near future – and it would be hopelessly optimistic to assume that there is the slightest chance of this happening – many of the fundamental problems would remain. The very pace of redevelopment destroys communities. Rapid mobility results in rootlessness. Social cohesion takes decades to establish; social dislocation comes in a few months with massive redevelopment. Old neighbours in streets and flats are gone for ever, the fragile advantages of close-knit family and social groupings are lost. Memories are mutilated, loneliness and isolation increase. Individuals and communities and institutions suffer as a result. Many of the residents in the inner-city are old. As the able young have left, the elderly have been abandoned. They lack a network of support.

The old familiar pattern of family life in working-class communities enabled people to overcome many personal problems. Care was in a family setting. Children were looked after by other members of the family in time of difficulty or when mothers needed to work. Such families formed the basis of natural human communities, which in turn serviced and maintained institutions and more formal groups. In many areas networks of families can be traced which provided the key members of a local church or a social club or a ward Labour Party. When such families were disrupted and moved, organizations collapsed and local leadership was dissipated. Unsurprisingly administrative solutions – shutting this church, amalgamating those social clubs, reorganizing local government and ward boundaries – have caused the situation to deteriorate still further. Many cities, London particularly so, are historically a collection of villages, and people live on a parochial scale. One 95-year-old lady who lived all her life in Borough High Street had never in the whole of her long life been half a mile to the north across London Bridge into London. In the part of

15

Southwark where we live it is amazing how often the question, 'Do you come from round here?' elicits the answer, 'No, I come from Camberwell,' or 'the Elephant' or 'Bermondsey' or other places within the radius of a mile. The reorganization of London into larger boroughs which have since been copied in many other local government reorganizations has resulted in boroughs which have no reality for their inhabitants. A borough with a quarter of a million inhabitants, one ward councillor for every four thousand inhabitants and four town halls is not on the right scale for a human community. Consequently people feel more cut off than ever from local politicians and local government officers, and feel more powerless than ever.

With the decline of the extended family and the indigenous community has come the rise of the helping agencies. Without a grandmother to look after children in crisis, more children are placed in care. Without a granddaughter to do the shopping, cook the meals and clean the house, more old people need home helps, meals on wheels, and nursing homes. Without a local father gathering together a few of his son's friends on a park for games, more youth workers are needed. With the collapse of local links and the breakdown of local information, more community workers are needed. At the same time, more of these professions are striving to become more efficient, to reduce amateur volunteers, and to improve their status, which means that local helpers are made to feel incompetent, unwanted and unnecessary.

As the extended family has declined owing to a lack of propinquity, so the nuclear family has come under increasing stress. In the inner-city areas the problems of marital discord, divorces, single-parent families and large families, loom large and have increased over the past few years. This breakdown in family life, especially the very frequent lack of an effective father, has intensified many of the inner-city problems, especially those connected with education and youth work.

The whole constellation of inner-city problems has been well illustrated in a study of inner-city Liverpool. It was found that there was a whole cluster of indices when a critical amount of social malaise had been reached. Areas with acute social malaise always contained a far higher than usual percentage of unskilled families, of acute overcrowding with an average exceeding 1·5 persons per room, and of large households. These areas could be easily identified because in them were found many crimes of theft, assault, burglary, and malicious damage, many unemployed debtors, many mentally ill adults and educationally sub-normal children, many deloused children. Many households had been served possession orders or Electricity Board entry warrants. In Liverpool it was found that these areas of acute social malaise were highest in the areas around the centre of the city, lowest in the private suburbs and higher again in the recent council estates on the outskirts of the city in Speke and Dovecote. The evidence from the survey substantiates the view that the inner residential areas contain a large proportion of the social problems of the city, and that the rehousing of people from these areas has done little to alleviate the problems that they face. The survey found that overcrowded housing and low economic status with its overtone of blighted educational opportunities are by far the most prominent factors associated with the distribution of social problems.

It is hardly surprising that the inner-city poor, being faced with such a multitude of inter-connected problems and disadvantages should be apathetic and disillusioned. Even when their neighbourhoods have been redeveloped they find their situation has changed only from disastrous to desperate. They have merely moved from a scabrous slum to a centrally heated ghetto. The speed with which new estates are vandalized and destroyed by their own residents shows that new homes alone cannot meet the manifest needs of their residents. Yet they know that as the proportion of owner-occupiers swells, it is unlikely that more resources will be diverted to those living in rented accommodation. Politics are concerned less with the needs of minorities than the wishes of majorities. One of the most surprising facts about British politics has been the respect for the law, the restraint, the gradualism, the low expectations, and the conservatism of the British working classes. It is difficult to understand how thousands upon thousands of people living in squalid slums with no hot water, no inside toilet, no bathrooms can tolerate a society which allows there to be new flats with many amenities including two bathrooms a mile or two away from the slums. The new flats are often bought by executives who already own a decent house elsewhere. It is difficult to understand how people can allow individual landowners to make profits of tens of millions of pounds by selling land at exorbitant prices which ensure that they and their children will never be able to afford to buy their own modest homes.

Such fatalistic behaviour by the inner-city residents springs from a belief that change cannot happen, that it will never come from the urban poor, and that their intellectual fellow-travellers are too few to affect the situation. Even the possibilities of improving their own living standard, of escaping from the ghetto, are often not achieved because differences in their social organizations and styles of life make it difficult. In urban areas money is spent more freely but saved less often. Capital accumulation does not take place. Bank accounts are not so common as the ubiquitous and practical loan club. Working people love trading, buying and selling. They enjoy markets and jumble sales. On average they give their children more pocket money than the middle classes, and conspicuous consumption at Christmas, weddings and parties of food and drink and gifts is especially noticeable. They buy cheap new goods, and replace them more often than the middle classes, saving far less, and making less provision for the future. Much of this is due to the sort of realization that a postman with four children is never going to be able to buy a house in London so he might as well rent a colour television and keep the family happy. People in poor and depressing circumstances need to spend money, to own something of which they can be proud – yet by over-spending they prolong their depressed state.

People in inner-city areas lack assurance and confidence. In their working lives they take orders rather than give them. In housing, welfare, education and health they receive benefits rather than distribute them. They obtain no credit for assertion, leadership, individualism and tackling problems. These qualities are seen as suspicious and likely to lead to trouble. They are trained to be inadequate, cowed by always being forced to ask for things, corrupted by thinking delegations to the Town Hall will solve problems because they have paid their rents. Tenants are unwilling to tackle social problems. Life is often hard and raw, and people are seldom prepared to go out on a limb for the general good, only for immediate and visible benefits. A child truanting from school, or breaking down and uprooting a roadside tree or breaking milk bottles in the road is not approached, questioned, diverted or reprimanded. He is simply ignored. Adults walk by, shunning involvement, hoping it will not happen near their homes. Such fatalism feeds on itself. It is self-perpetuating. Council spokesmen know that participation means more work, more confrontations, more delays, and so resist communication and partnership. Officials state that it will serve no useful purpose to inform people at this point about decisions or developments concerning their present or future homes or schools. People feel inferior, act inferior, are thus thought to be inferior, and treated as inferior. As one man sadly summarized it, 'You know, I do not think they think we are intelligent enough. You trust those what's like you.'

The accumulation of problems in the inner-city is formidable. Inadequate housing, poor health, bad education, low income, a depressing environment, lack of space, few amenities, coupled with the breakdown of family and community life, and a mood of apathy and hopelessness present a dispiriting townscape. It is a depressing panorama with remarkable similarities in the cities of Western Europe and North America, a picture which is repeating itself in growing areas elsewhere in the world. Most of the statistics and examples are taken from the British Isles, but the reality is the same in the United States, France or Germany. Yet for the people who live and dwell in the inner-city their vision is of a microcosm, not macrocosm. They live in a small area, often restricted by lack of adequate transport to spending most of their lives in one tiny conglomeration of streets or tenements. They are in a community based on a place, when many others have joined a community based on mutual interests and not immediate geographical locality. So the inner-city cannot be effectively studied nor solutions to its problems found solely in a global or national context. Much of this book consists in examining what is happening, looking at those solutions that have been attempted in one small area of the inner-city in the north of the London Borough of Southwark. Before it can be studied, however, its historical determinants

19

must be analysed, for the deprivation of the inner-city areas stretches far back into the past. Without an understanding of the roots and development of the deprivation, it is not possible to discover how it can be changed.

2. The Growth of the Ghetto

South London existed from the time of the Domesday Book to Tudor times as open fields surrounding small villages on the outskirts of London. Even when these villages lay only two or three miles from the City of London they had little contact with it apart from supplying fresh produce to the city inhabitants.

After the sixteenth century there came signs of suburban growth. They were described in early Stuart times as 'suburbs of London which are inhabited for the greater part by an inept population of the lowest description'. Gradually a more mixed population became established, although unlike small towns the suburbs were never occupied by completely diverse social classes. By 1710 regular mail deliveries had been extended to a radius of ten miles from the London General Post Office. From then until the middle of the eighteenth century there begins a general exodus of the richer middle classes to the suburbs, within five miles of St. Paul's. In South London this migration was aided and speeded by improvements to the roads and, crucially, to bridge-building. In 1750 Westminster Bridge was built; in 1769 Blackfriars. The prospering middle classes built villas and large houses and went by coach to the city from which they had fled in search of suburban respectability, away from the repulsive aspects of central city life, the polluted air, foul water and overcrowded housing. Their flight reflected their increased sensitivity to urban environment. The suburbs, the decentralized part of the city to which they are inextricably linked by economic and social ties, are seen from the eighteenth century as middle-class purlieus, insulated from the city and its poorer inhabitants in their congested streets. Yet despite the rapid growth of the suburbs before Victorian times this expansion paled into insignificance before the urbanization in the nineteenth century. London grew as had no city in the world before it. Not only did the national population grow from eleven million in 1801 to thirty-eight million in 1901, but it changed from predominantly rural population to an over-whelmingly urban one. The staggering growth of London was a result – from 865,000 people in 1801 to 4,500,000 in 1901. In our own area, the St. George's Ward in Camberwell grew from an average density in 1841 of 25 people to the acre to 148 to the acre in 1901, the people coming mostly from rural areas of England or Ireland. As they came the suburban migration continued. Booth wrote, 'The district became steadily poorer as the fairly comfortable moved south, and immigrants from Walworth arrive'. Masterman at the end of the Victorian era commented, 'Above in trains, or below in undergrounds the suburban middle classes journey across the living world of the masses whom they distrust as being a red threat.'

As the armies of the workers advanced so the suburban masses beat a tactical retreat. The suburbs of yesterday became the slums of today. The isolation of the poor was a corollary of the rise of the middle-class suburbs whose geographical in-sularity was the symbol of a more fundamental social and political separation.

This huge growth of homes and population in the inner suburbs in Victorian times was a response to the vast population growth, but it was enabled and facilitated by other factors. Transport continued to improve so workers could get to work by other means than on foot. From the 1830's the omnibus service grew so that by 1860 buses were running every five minutes from the city to Camberwell Green. While the service increased in regularity it halved in price to come within reach of the better paid clerks and artisans. Railways and trams replaced omnibuses from the 1860's. The cheap tram fares and the working man's special railway fares led to the breakdown of the financial and geographical isolation of the inner suburbs and their invasion by the working classes (many of whom had had their slum homes destroyed by the building of the railways and better roads).

Yet despite all the cheap travel most people worked locally as businesses moved to the suburbs drawn by the availability of labour and the better rail, road and canal transport.

As well as by cheap transport, the suburban growth was aided by the easy availability of capital for housebuilding and the relatively cheap land which meant that even for the poorer people houses – albeit cheap terraced houses – were generally built. Relatively few tenement blocks were erected as they were less private and more expensive. The inner-city suburbs were built by speculative builders who, aided by the development of piped water and mains sewage, provided homes infinitely preferable to the slums the city workers had left behind.

The condition of Central London in the mid-century was appalling, a 'great, foul city, rattling, growling, smoking, stinking, ghastly heap of fermenting brickwork, pouring out poison at every pore,' as Ruskin described it. In 1842 Robert Warner, a Quaker teetotaller, had his insurance premium increased because drinking the water in London was such a health hazard. The insurance companies' financial acumen was shown when there came another of the bad cholera outbreaks, mainly as a result of the green-black, stinking, sewer-polluted Thames and the unnumbered cesspits, rotting privies and overcrowded burial grounds. Over 400 a day died in the slums. By 1871 all sewers were covered and by the end of the century piped water for all was available, with the houses having water closets and piped gas as well.

So by the end of the nineteenth century there had been tremendous progress in dealing with the huge migration to the city. There was better housing, better health, better transport, better pay for workers with shorter hours and more security, and fewer central slums. Improved schooling came as a result of the establishment of the new Board schools. There was less crime, as the once poorly paid and often assaulted police gradually reduced the violence and robberies. There were fewer beggars, ragpickers, homeless, sewer-scavengers, fewer illegitimate children, fewer prostitutes (over 100,000 in 1860, mostly under thirteen), brothels and opium dens.

Yet of course there were enormous exceptions to the rule, and there was massive poverty and appalling conditions for many. Many workers were grossly overworked and underpaid, living in overcrowded, dirty lodging houses or as sub-tenants. Huge

23

areas degenerated from meadow to slum in a generation. One was in our immediate area. The Bowyer-Smiths lived in a fine mansion near Camberwell Road. They leased their land in 1781 to William Austin for meadow land. But because of the incompetent drawing up of the lease, the land was subdivided, and by the middle of the nineteenth century Sultan Street was a mess of sheds, glue-factories, cowsheds, piggeries and houses. It filled with Irish immigrants, petty crooks and unfortunates. Booth in 1899 found over twenty people in six-roomed houses living in dire poverty. Many of the houses had secret exits to facilitate their inhabitants' escaping from the police visitations. It was a citadel of outcasts.

Open land grew increasingly scarce as the houses covered the land. By 1899 there was little open ground left for recreation, and an L.C.C. conference on Open Space in that year called the area between Camberwell Green and the Thames 'the blackest spot for open space in the whole of London'. The Borough of Southwark had less than thirty-four acres of open space, less than one square yard per inhabitant. The danger was not recognized until it was too late. No efforts at preservation were made until the 1866 Metropolitan Commons Act, and by then the inner-city was built over.

There were also the ever present contrasts between the areas occupied by the urban poor and those occupied by the prosperous middle classes. Even the choice of trees had social overtones. There were planes and horse chestnuts for the wide avenues and lofty mansions of the rich; limes, laburnums and acacias for the middle classes, and unadorned macadam for the wage-earners.

Even religion was class-orientated. In 1876 a reporter of the *South London Observer* wrote at the opening of St. Jude's, Peckham: 'At last Peckham can boast of a Church of England where the poor can go and say their prayers without living in terror of the pew rent collectors.'

Schools were more rigidly class-orientated than churches. The middle classes paid over ten pounds a year to educate their young at Dulwich College, or Alleyn's or Mary Datchelor's. Grammar schools often became fee-paying schools in the Victorian era while the poor spent less than two pounds a year to send their children to religious schools. Finally came the Board schools, built after the 1870's to catch the young who went to no school. These huge schools often catered for a thousand children with up to eighty in each class.

All the historical background emphasizes the deprivation of the urban poor. They moved into South London from rural areas. They faced a brutal struggle for survival – medical, economic and social. There was at first no sense of roots, of continuity or community. The middle classes moved away as the urban poor moved in. The control of local affairs was progressively eroded throughout the nineteenth century. Owing to the needs of efficiency, local government structure got larger and thus more distant. The powers of the old vestry, and its acrimonious arguments about local affairs, were reduced from 1834 when highway control, police, sewage, lighting and poor law relief were taken from them. Their remaining powers were whittled away throughout the century.

The poor could only react to events, never influence or control them. They reacted gratefully to some, such as rises in living accommodation standards, and bitterly to others, but they could seldom control anything.

They had (contrary to popular belief) little sense of community involvement and belonging. It was, when it existed, a united sense of common deprivation. It was a street community. The street was where the main markets, entertainments, and the children's playgrounds existed. Even taverns were secondary to streets. Where there was one tavern for every 160 people in 1837 there was only one for every 845 people in 1902.

They had no stake in the area. Even in the early twentieth century when the community spirit was strongest, when fewest people had moved and immigration had ceased, the sense of identity was not based on anything they owned, whether houses or schools, but on their mutual deprivation. Constantly the best emigrated. Their leaving created a ghetto for those who could not depart.

It is difficult not to admire the way in which the Victorians dealt with the vast growth of London during the nineteenth century. With enormous problems and an unprecedented situation

25

they radically improved the general lot of the people over the course of the century despite the vast natural growth of population and the rural influx. It would be churlish to deny the advances. Yet some of the progress resulted in disabilities such as the loss of the vestige of local democratic control and the vanishing open spaces. The gap between the middle classes and the urban poor gaped as wide as ever. Both were lifted by the rising tide of Victorian prosperity, but the middle classes were lifted earlier, and then lifted higher. The space between the two groups failed to close over the century. It may even have widened as hostility grew with increasing geographical isolation. Even with all the improvements, at the end of the nineteenth century, South London could not be regarded as a pleasant or rewarding place to live. It was described in 1899 by Besant as, 'A city without a municipality, it has no newspapers, no university, no intellectual, artistic, scientific, musical, literary centre, no clubs, no public buildings. Its central edifice was a public house, the Elephant and Castle.'

The inner-city area in which we live had its main outlines determined during the Victorian times. Its previous history was buried by the end of the nineteenth century. Since then it is surprising how little changed for the next fifty years. Our particular part of South London is situated in a triangle lying between three main roads, with its corners marked by the Elephant and Castle, Kennington Oval and Camberwell Green. Much of the area still consists of Victorian terraces, or tenements, usually in poor condition, while the rest of the properties are council flats and maisonettes which are gradually replacing the older properties. There is very little privately owned property in the area – less than 2%. Most people live either in council flats or privately rented homes, a substantial proportion of which is owned by the Victorian charitable trusts which erected them. The total area is about 400 acres, and the population is about 25,000 which as a result of rebuilding has declined from its peak of about 50,000 sixty years ago. There is little industry in the area, and most of it is grouped under or alongside the railway line; however, most employment is fairly local. Many women do cleaning, either early morning in offices or evening in schools. The men work in service industries, as car mechanics, bus drivers, postmen, electricians; or they are dockers, printers, building or office workers. There is growing unemployment, especially for unqualified school leavers. Many of the traditional employers, the docks, food-processing industries, and the printing industry are moving further out of London, continuing the symbiosis of labour and industry noted in Victorian times.

The area was extensively bombed during the war as a result of which all the four Anglican churches in the area have been rebuilt. The bombs destroyed not only churches but much housing, which has stimulated massive council rebuilding. This area in which we live and work is a fairly typical inner-city area. It does not have worse social conditions than any other. It is different only as all localities are different.

What it does show, and this is common to all inner-city areas, is the consequence of its historical and present deprivation, a desperate situation which is not improving and which may well be deteriorating. Poverty and deprivation are relative concepts. You are poor compared to somebody else's wealth. One of the most depressing recent developments in the inner-city has been the increasing realization that not only are its inhabitants poor compared to the evidence of wealth which is paraded before them in papers and on television, but also that the chances of bridging the gap between wealth and poverty are declining.

They know that the poorest third of the population has less than one sixth of the total national post tax income, a proportion which has remained almost unchanged for the past quarter of a century. They know that the poorest half of the country, the nine million poorest households jointly own less than the richest 90,000 families. Each of the rich families owns on average one hundred times as much as those in the poorer half of the population. The discrepancies are far greater when the really poor in the inner-cities are compared with the rich. Every disadvantage of the inner-city has its parallel advantage in the rich suburbs or country homes of the affluent. With their good housing, good education, good amenities, abundant space, adequate wealth, these self-confident communities are the reverse side of the inner-city deprivation. None is attainable by the majority of inner-city inhabitants. Few of them will show sufficient social mobility to join the ranks of even the comfortably off. They know that with high land and house prices, with educational qualifications being demanded for more and more good jobs, they and their children are never likely to escape, and such knowledge saps the energy, morale and confidence of all but the most resilient.

No analysis of the situation in the inner-city today can avoid the conclusion that the position is critical owing both to the constellation of problems environmental, historical, and human, and to the ignorance of the situation amongst the more privileged dwellers in suburban homes. They are cut off from the urban ghettos by location, employment, education and class. No city can survive without a reasonable distribution of differing trades, skills and social mixing. Yet in many cities today, the poorly paid building workers, nurses, transport workers, postmen and others are unable to find decent accommodation in which to live and raise their families. The gradual drift of the most able inhabitants in the inner-city out of their own localities means that those who remain are the oldest, worst educated, least ambitious members of the community.

It is hoped that a recognition of the serious nature of the problems will generate the will to solve them. Otherwise the future holds little but the prospect of a polarized group at the lowest end of the social spectrum, a poor, deprived group, which is under-educated, under-skilled and relatively unemployable. It will be a group increasingly envious of the great majority who enjoy education, skills, and secure and interesting jobs. They will be sullen and apathetic and occasionally violent, an agglomeration which will display above average indices of mental disturbance, family break-up and petty disturbance of the social order. It will place totally disproportionate demands on welfare and remedial sources, and will be the urban problems of the future.

Already there is in existence at the core of all large cities a landscape bedevilled by massive problems yet alien to the suburban majority. It is ignored, misunderstood and discriminated against, an urban ghetto whose almost impenetrable walls have grown up steadily over the decades, and whose solidity is enhanced by their invisibility. This ghetto poisons the life not merely of its inhabitants, but also of the society of which it is a part. It can only be destroyed, and its inhabitants incorporated into a wider and more healthy society, by a massive and radical change both from outside and inside its walls.

3. The Failure of Professionals

The working classes in the inner-city suffer from a multitude of disadvantages which result from the history, social organization, political and financial weakness of the urban poor. These disadvantages have accelerated the decline of leadership and the growth of fatalistic apathy which preclude any gradual amelioration in the urban ghetto. These disadvantages have been accentuated by the decline in community morale in the inner-city. The future holds little but the prospect of a further depletion of the residual leaders as the more able members of the community desert the urban ghetto which will shrink in dimensions but become more recalcitrant in nature. It will therefore be dismissed by those outside its walls as a hopeless situation best dealt with by a policy of benign neglect. Meanwhile inside the ghetto we can expect less social and political activists as more people attempt to compensate for their powerlessness with the vicarious excitement of gladiatorial football conflicts or the bland entertainment emanating from their television sets.

The only remedy for the situation is rapid social change. This must be based on a renewal of political will to eradicate the evils of the inner-city. Such fundamental change will inevitably mean a massive redistribution of wealth and resources and a positive discrimination in favour of the inner-city at the expense of the outer suburbs. Such a policy of rapid social change needs leadership, and there is no shortage of candidates who claim to be in a position to initiate such change. Many groups of people have tried and are trying to alter the present situation.

Education

One of the earliest and most persistent agencies for change has been teachers and educationalists. At least one hundred

30

years ago it was realized that it was impossible to expect an illiterate and inarticulate group of people rapidly to change their social status. Compulsory education was introduced to enable children living in the inner-city areas to share the educational opportunities of other children living in more favoured environments.

Yet from the beginning there were gross differences between children crammed eighty to a class in the Board schools, and the middle-class private schools of the suburbs. The children of the urban poor were being educated in a different way, at different schools, for different ends, from the children of the middle classes. Whatever the intentions, the educational system has perpetuated and strengthened the class system. The leaders have come from the private schools, the managers from the grammar schools, and the workers from the secondary schools. The percentage of children from working-class homes entering university has hardly changed in the past fifty years.

As this became more and more obvious, and was stressed in a plethora of reports – Newsom, Plowden and Crowther – the emphasis has changed. Rather than attempting to select bright children at eleven, and training the rest to be the artificers of society, the emphasis has been placed on comprehensive schooling to give all children an equal chance.

However, educational equality of opportunity has proved an elusive myth. Private schools and selective grammar schools siphon off a disproportionate amount of talent and money, making true comprehensive schooling an untried ideal. Also it is almost impossible for working-class children to overcome their educational disadvantages. Even in egalitarian Sweden, with totally comprehensive education, with a uniform pattern of teaching, and a rigidly allocated system of facilities, far more middle-class than working-class children obtain university places.

In England at a primary level the research by the National Children's Bureau showed that at the age of seven all the measures of both ability and attainment show a sharp difference between the children of fathers with manual and non-manual occupations. The introduction of more freedom, team-teaching, family groupings and play-orientated methods has paradoxically worsened the situation of the inner-city children. While the

31

more self-disciplined middle-class child has embraced the new educational ideas, the working-class child has often been confused and lost. The children from inner-city homes are less socialized, act out their aggressions, have received less guidance and direction, and have less control over their behaviour. They find it difficult to exercise choice without guidance and information. The schools they go to have a far higher proportion of severely disturbed children with extreme behavioural problems, and thus tend to be less disciplined than suburban schools. In their primary schools they meet young teachers who have learnt at their training colleges that the aims of teaching are to allow children to grow as individuals, to respect children and their ways of thinking. Yet young working-class children are less able to respond to such a liberal regime than middle-class children. The guidance they receive is tentative, the experiences on which they are supposed to build are incoherent. In many inner-city primary schools the children become bored and rebellious, the teachers threatened and frightened.

By the age of eleven the working-class child in the inner-city area has fallen still further behind his suburban rival. His best chance would have come with a directive and authoritarian teaching. He has received the opposite. The pattern continues in the secondary schools. Comprehensive schools in England are neighbourhood schools, and in inner-city areas that means schools with pupils drawn from a very restricted social class. The children have low expectations of themselves, expectations which are constantly verified by experience. They feel deprived, unskilled, valueless, unloved. They act out their anxieties and aggression with few restraints. They feel, rightly, that their education will not help their material prosperity. Teachers dislike teaching such unacademic and unmotivated children. Schools with up to 1800 children have difficulties in building and organizing children into small communities. It is easy to have a good comprehensive school in a good socially mixed area, but desperately difficult in an inner-city area. The speedy disappearance of grammar schools simply ensures that a yet smaller proportion of children will reach any form of higher education. The children, intellectually forced in the grammar school greenhouses, will not be pressured in the unstreamed comprehensives. In the competition for scarce higher educational resources, the more thrusting middle-class children from private, grammar, and suburban comprehensive schools will succeed. The inner-city child will fail. The rapid closure of grammar schools, and the swift spread of unstreamed, mixed-ability teaching in comprehensives will accentuate an already desperate situation. The large numbers of antiquated school buildings hardly ease the problem, nor does the shortage of experienced teachers in the inner-city. While suburban and country schools are overwhelmed with applications for teaching posts by hordes of teachers, especially primary teachers, it has been a desperate problem in inner-city schools to get any staff no matter how poor. Even when staff are available they are usually young and inexperienced teachers who are starting their careers in the city. In a few years they will move out of the city schools owing to the long hours of travelling and the virtual impossibility of obtaining homes near inner-city schools. The greatest shortage of staff is in those of ability and experience aged between thirty and fifty.

As a result of the deprived background of the children, the old buildings, the staffing difficulties and the inappropriate teaching methods, the children have few academic results on which to pride themselves. They learn neither useful skills nor self-confidence with which to face an often hostile world when they leave school. Like Mark Twain they could aptly if bitterly comment, 'We never let our schooling interfere with our education.'

Any idea that teachers or schools will be able to bring about ideal change in the inner-city is illusory. So desperate is the situation that not only did the General Secretary of the National Union of Teachers forecast that London's education will soon be the worst in the country, but local inspectors also admit that inner-city education is worse now than forty years ago. Worst of all many teachers are simply giving up the struggle to provide any total, meaningful or sane values and standards. They are advocating what amounts to a boycott of the traditional examination-orientated educational structure. They teach whatever bores the children least. As one inner-city headmaster of a large comprehensive school expressed it, 'If the children do not wish to learn something we do not believe it is worth teaching'. So the schools undertake vocational training, woodwork, metalwork, craft studies, needlework and housecrafts. They try to base their academic studies on the cultural affinities of the neighbourhood, teaching maths through football pools and league tables, English through discussion of television serials, and music through pop records. To some extent this works. One local comprehensive had to shut its car repair shop for a time as it was used by pupils for repairing and respraying stolen cars! Yet working-class culture can easily degenerate through cheap literature and banal pop songs into violence and sadism. Even if such attempts keep the children contented, and the huge numbers of truants make this seem unlikely, it inevitably means that they will leave school without the skills and abilities and qualifications which society demands from those who live outside the urban ghetto. More unemployment is to be found among the young unskilled people in the inner-city than among any other age group in any area. In 1975 hundreds of thousands of school leavers could not find any jobs. The last in and the first out of any jobs are the uneducated and the unskilled. There are fewer and fewer jobs available for the uneducated young in the inner-city. Even when they do get jobs, they find their schools have only trained them for life in the ghetto.

The Political Parties

Another agency which has constantly claimed and attempted to achieve rapid change has been the political parties. It is obvious that only through political action can the resources of men and money be diverted into the ghettos, so this was to be expected. Unsurprisingly, the Conservative Party has not been a power in inner-city areas during this century, although it usually obtains some 20% of the working-class vote. In many areas it has virtually no grass roots organization, and is seen by the vast majority of voters as the party of the rich oppressors. The Communists work enormously hard, and have a small band of immensely dedicated workers who toil away in unions, in tenants' groups and any other spheres of influence that they can discover. They are, however, viewed with immense suspicion by the traditionally minded working-class voters in the inner-city areas. They very rarely win seats even on the local council, and seldom garner as many votes as the Conservatives. The Liberals are a more fluctuating and interesting case. Up to very recently their only areas of strength were in the Celtic fringes of Britain, and in some disenchanted suburban seats, but they have recently been broadening their appeal. They have captured more rural, farming seats in England, and held one inner-city seat in Birmingham Ladywood for a short time. Perhaps more importantly than Parliamentary seats, they have been capturing many local government citadels including the city of Liverpool. They have been the first of the major parties to campaign on the slogan 'Community Politics', and represent the only real attempt to concentrate on burning local issues and allow local figures to represent people in elections. However, despite these encouraging straws in the wind, they are woefully weak in most inner-city areas, and until 1974 found it almost impossible to find candidates, let alone supporters and voters. Whether they can overcome the inherent inertia in British political life and continue expansion, or whether they will repeatedly dwindle again as the battle for power at the general elections looms is an open and fascinating question.

Political life in most inner metropolitan areas means the Labour Party. Every political office in each area is held or controlled by the local Labour Party, and often has been for decades. All the real political struggles take place inside the local Labour Party. This is not automatically disastrous, but it tends towards political apathy and domination by small cliques. The London Borough of Southwark, for example, displays a fairly typical political scene. Three Labour Members of Parliament and Labour representatives exist on the Greater London Council. Fifty-eight of the sixty Borough councillors are Labour members. Yet the local party is woefully weak. An average ward will have 12,000 voters yet only a third of those will vote in local elections, and Southwark in its 1972 by-election had one of the lowest turnouts in British political history, only 30% of the electorate bothering to vote. The local Labour ward party will have about 100 members out of the 12,000 voters, of whom about ten will attend the monthly ward meeting. Of these ten people two or three will be sitting councillors and most of the others will be pensioners. Candidates for political office will be selected by about twenty people at a ward meeting. Any newcomers to the ward meeting will be subjected to a trial by boredom (arguably a good preparation for participation in local government). Anything new – faces, ideas, accents – will be viewed with grave suspicion. Blind, octogenarian councillors have been selected instead of eager, competent tenants' leaders. The tribal succession goes to the longest-serving and oldest candidate.

In practice the political life of a local ward depends on two or three local families and their friends, and they are so busy trying to prevent the organization from seizing up that they have few spare moments to study new ideas or initiatives. People who know nothing about education are selected to school management boards on their first visit to a local ward meeting because there is just no one else to do the chore. In such a situation rule is by a self-perpetuating oligarchy.

This system has thrown up several excellent leaders. Yet there remain the almost paranoid fear and suspicion of outsiders, especially professional, educated outsiders. Members of the Southwark Labour Party fear that such men, Fabian university lecturers with Marxist leanings, will take over Southwark. They are believed to have captured the national Labour Party as well as London Boroughs such as Camden, Newham or neighbouring Lambeth. It is no coincidence that the only non-graduate Cabinet member in the 1966-70 Labour Government was Southwark's Member Ray Gunter. But neither is it a coincidence that he was one of the most traditional members of the Cabinet. For the fact is that a London Borough, like any administrative area in local government, is difficult to administer. It has a budget of millions of pounds, a staff of thousands, and it is unrealistic to expect men and women with little formal education, few professional qualifications, and scant administrative experience effectively to control such a large enterprise. In practice these part-time councillors are forced to lean overheavily on the advice of their officers who in practice control the borough and the lives of its inhabitants. No real or radical change is likely to come from our present political apparatus.

Architects and Planners

Another group of professionals whose endeavours result in the most manifold and visible changes in the inner-city environments are the architects and planners working for the local authorities. Despite their rigid professional standards, despite their enormous recent opportunities for transforming the local townscape, they have been perhaps the most blameworthy for the bleak and barbarous blocks with which they have littered the city. Like all groups of professionals they are imprisoned by underlying social trends they did not create, the trend towards gigantism, towards inhumanly large estates built of the cheapest materials, of housing yardstick cost limitations and a lack of building manpower, materials and money. It has not been the architects' and planners' fault that their political masters have not been able to decide whether or not to build homes to high standards to meet higher space requirements and changing leisure habits. This would result in lower densities, higher costs and fewer buildings. The alternative is to attempt to clear the backlog of the queues of homeless with the certainty of building flats which will be despised and rejected less than half way through their lives. The Aylesbury estate in Southwark was called a slum on its official opening day. Yet the architects and planners have been responsible for colossal blunders as a result of their arrogance, by their inability to react to the pace of change, and by their utter failure to comprehend the world of their true clients, those who will live in the homes and the estates they build.

Their professional arrogance has resulted in their ignoring advice from those who warned that their pursuit of new materials, shapes and theories were based on a paucity of research. Their failure to discern changing social trends meant they were designing fire-places when central-heating was expanding and coal merchants going bankrupt. They were not providing garages while residents were buying cars. They were failing to design play areas while the bomb sites were disappearing and the streets in which the children played were filling with traffic. Their inability to consult their clients meant that they designed homes that were too small, too cramped, too

37

inflexible, too uniform, homes that are approached by too many stairs or along corridors or in inadequate lifts. They have seen people as a commodity to be packaged and boxed. By ignoring the prevalence of crime, vandalism and noise in the inner-city they have failed to provide real privacy in homes while paradoxically providing few areas for communication. New estates have no wells, no communal wash-houses, no street markets. The tenements are surrounded not by parks or woods, gardens or playgrounds, but by expanses of grass littered with detritus and guarded by the gloomy and ineffectual signs reading, 'No Ball Games By Order of the Council'. The planners and architects have utterly failed to predict, and thus to improve, the social environment, the world of the planned. They have filled estates with families with many young children, and have then been surprised by vandalism and neglect. Their names are writ in concrete.

Social Workers, Doctors and Police

Another group of professionals who have attempted to change the present situation has been the social caseworkers. These have attempted to improve the situation by giving individual help to the many people who have broken under the strain of life in the urban environment. There are many more social workers in the inner-city than in the suburbs or country. Over 2,500 people work in the Social Services Department of the London Borough of Southwark. This is partly a result of the breakdown in family and community relationships, with the vacuum being filled by statutory agencies, and partly of the urban aid programmes.

As a result of the Seebohm report, area teams of social workers were established in the early 1970's with no more chaos and confusion than attended Napoleon's retreat from Moscow. The aim was to bring the social services closer to their clients, and most area teams advertised their presence widely asking people to bring their problems to them. Unsurprisingly in the leaderless and disturbed areas they came and came and came. The social services were and are totally unable to cope. The staff turnover in inner-city areas became horrific, the administration was sporadic, and the workers almost ceased to do casework. They simply rushed around, or more accurately phoned around, in a vain attempt to supply the home helps, mental hostel beds, accommodation for homeless families, and child care residential beds that are again simply inadequate to cope with the needs and demands. The social workers in area teams have ceased to be men and women giving care, consideration and counselling to those who need it. They are more like firemen rushing from one conflagration to another trying desperately to eke out an inadequate supply of water. Even when they have time for casework, because they act as mothers and fathers to clients who have regressed to child-like dependency, they are in grave danger of stifling initiative, of becoming social aspirins.

The situation of workers for voluntary agencies is different. The statutory agencies have no time, energy or personnel to examine the situation or to reform it. The voluntary agencies are closer to the ground. They have not so systematically destroyed the service by professionalizing it. The workers fill in the many gaps – the legal aid gap, the Council of Social Services gap, the addicts and alcoholism gap, the single homeless gap. It is difficult for the voluntary agencies to co-ordinate over the whole field. They are too specialized to obtain an overall view or to plan an overall strategy.

Another profession which works in the inner-city areas is that of the doctors. They have the potential to change the situation, but have as yet shown little desire to do so. They also exemplify the tendency to move away from the inner-city areas, there being few who continue both to live and work in the district. While they are generally highly regarded, they are usually so busy dealing with medical crises that they do not have much time to examine the underlying problems of the inner-city, despite the close relevance to their professional work. Just as working-class areas have more than their fair share of educational problems, so they have more than their rightful amount of medical difficulties. There is a correlation between class and illness even when industrial diseases like lead poisoning are excluded. One of the few medical advantages of inner-city areas is that industrial workers are not nearly as obese as suburban office-workers. Recently hospitals have been setting up Departments of Community Medicine to study such correlations and to initiate research into how the health of whole communities can be improved.

The police are among the most controversial of the professionals working in the inner-city. Opinions vary violently as to whether they are the only defence against anarchy and urban warfare, or whether they are venal and vindictive towards the urban poor among whom they work. Of all the professional groups they are perhaps closest in social ranking to the local residents, and while it is undeniable that they despise the poor, the young who commit up to 75% of the crimes, and especially the blacks, there seems little real evidence that they are widely corrupt. The re-establishment of the local beat policeman is one of the few examples of a large organization reversing the trend towards remote and centralized, if highly trained, professional services.

Professional and Other Helping Agencies

There are several common problems and disadvantages from which the majority of professional groups working in the inner-city suffer, and there are of course many professions which have not been included in this brief survey. These disadvantages vitiate and even negate the progress they strive to achieve.

The first is that they are working in an extremely difficult situation with many problems which are not of their causing, and which they have little power to overcome. Many of these were mentioned in the first chapter.

Secondly, they are often desperately undermanned, and also suffer from rapid staff turnover. While they need the best staff possible they find it difficult to attract them. It is much easier to teach in a competitively orientated, academic suburban grammar or comprehensive school than in a school which finds it extremely difficult to get the children to the classroom and keep them there. Teachers have to prevent children from vandalizing the building, and to hold the children who are well below average in educational attainments (none of whom will ever leave with reputable qualifications). Most of the other professional workers can have a much easier life elsewhere. Add to

40

this the time and expense of travelling daily from the suburbs, the near impossibility of buying or renting accommodation in the inner-city, and it is not surprising that most professional workers in the inner-city are either young and easily disillusioned idealists doing a brief tenure of work or those who find it difficult to get as good a job elsewhere. From firemen to hospital staff, to teachers to planners, to midwives to property valuers to public health inspectors, the cry goes up from both the professions and the service trades that they are undermanned and cannot obtain the experienced staff they need to cope with the problems they face.

Thirdly, due to the fact (already mentioned) that they do not live in their area of work, they are seen – unfairly – as exploiters who drive into the area from outside, for they do not share in its life outside their narrow, specialized roles. They work from nine to five (usually the worst hours for the people wanting to see them) and then drive away with a sigh of relief to their pleasant suburban homes. They are viewed as rulers, those who have decided social priorities, as the new imperialists. In extreme urban situations like New York's Harlem, social workers and teachers are lumped together with the police as representatives of the establishment. They become scapegoats for an intolerable existence. Without deriding their professionalism, it must be said that there is an experience of what life in an area is like which can only be gained through a long immersion in its total existence. Only by living in the midst of an area for many years, shopping in the same shops, having one's children attending the same schools, youth clubs and playgroups as other children, chafing under the common disadvantages and enjoying the common advantages, can one gain a significant and unified picture of the society one is hoping to mould and influence. This is especially true when one's own background and upbringing was in a vastly different situation. Too often professional workers do not discover from or co-operate with those who reside there.

Finally, they suffer from the disadvantage that the larger the role they play the more they reduce the powers of local residents to exercise leadership. They create increased dependency by the very skill with which they use their professional abilities.

41

However democratic their ideals may be, in practice they are paid by, and thus ultimately responsible to the local council, or the educational authority or the central governmental agency, and not directly to the local people they are supposed to serve. Their acceptance of advice from local people is therefore always a personal decision which can be rescinded when there is a clash of viewpoints.

Unfortunately, an apathetic and fatalistic local populace lacking education, power and leadership is made more dependent and leaderless as the number of professional workers from statutory agencies pouring into the district increases. It is a bleak diagnosis. But there *are* examples of organizations, professional groups and individuals who can provide skills, train leaders and comprehend through immersion in the district its manifold needs and problems, its weaknesses and strengths. The oldest of these professions, working for the oldest of the organizations, is the clergy of the Christian church.

The local church in the inner-city is indigenous. It is controlled and to a large extent financed by its local members who provide much of its leadership. The clergy always reside in their parishes, usually for many years at a time. They are responsible to, and paid by local residents.

The local church has inherited large amounts of plant, not just the church building itself, but also halls and houses for the clergy to live in, and often other meeting rooms, youth club premises, church schools and other buildings. It has been frequently suggested that the church should divest itself of its buildings, and become once again the nomadic church free from encumbrances which tie an institution down with chains of material self-interest to a particular culture. Yet the availability of building plant can be an immense asset. Most inner-city areas have few meeting places for social activities or where small groups or committees can meet. Yet without meeting places communities cannot grow, and the churches are often the only bodies in the inner-city which can provide such facilities. Its resources of buildings as well as professional help can easily be put at the service of local groups. It can serve as the host. Its halls can be, and often are used for meetings of local tenants' and residents' groups, for confrontations with local councillors, to question or challenge prospective political candidates whether for the local council or for parliamentary office. The candidates can learn the issues which concern their prospective constituents. The voters can assess their representative's capabilities. The halls can be used as places where local headmasters and educationalists are confronted with the defects and dereliction of local schools, where doctors can be questioned by their patients, where dances can be held or socials or jumble sales or whatever is required to bring enjoyment and enlightenment. It is fortunate that the churches in the inner-city have resisted the temptations of most organizations to sell their properties so that offices, shopping centres or car parks could be built on the land.

Just as the church has gained considerable scope from the retention of its inner-city buildings, so it has from retaining its priests. Their professional independence has given them considerable freedom to denounce oppression as they see and find it in a way that is not possible for most public figures. They can give a respected lead in difficult situations, for they are well-known local figures. Their children *do* go to local schools. They and their wives shop at nearby shops. They share in the pains and pleasures of local people at hours of the day and night. They relate to a highly heterogeneous collection of people at many different levels. They meet local social workers and attend the wedding festivities of local families. Thus they meet people at the great rites of passage during their lives, when babies are born, couples wed, during the mourning for the dead. They are not occasional visitors but neighbours and friends, a situation and relationship of far greater equality and intimacy than that of distant professionals.

They are the servants of their local churches, and thus set in the largest and liveliest groups in the inner-city, groups integral to their area yet part of a national and international body. Church congregations, though small, are far larger and more effective than any other formal inner-city community or group. They contain the whole range of ages and abilities and intellects. Many of their members are the most concerned and active members of the community, and are often tenants' leaders, run playgroups and organize pressure groups in their wider communities. They are also people bound together by common beliefs, standards and values, which contradict the structures of class divisiveness, social privilege and financial exploitation in which they find themselves. Thus the clergy and the local churches are in a unique position to provide leadership which can change and transform the urban ghettos in which they are situated.

The churches and the clergy are not the only organization and professional workers striving to transform the inner-city from the inside rather than the outside. There remain many university and school settlements in the inner-city, founded by Victorian philanthropic bodies often with a directly missionary purpose. Many of these, like the churches, have a large amount of available buildings. If they lack an immediate rapport with the local populace, they often provide a body of professional workers living in properties owned by settlements. One group of workers centred on the settlements is the community workers. Community work is a new discipline that has emerged in the last decade, and many other agencies – churches, schools, social and youth workers – have added a community-work element to their work. The community-development approach has sprung out of a realization that in a complex society you cannot merely help individuals on an exclusive basis, ignoring their families, neighbours and surrounding community. In a sick community there will be few healthy individuals. So community workers attempt to restore sick communities to health, especially in inner-city areas where they have been speedily degenerating.

They have achieved a great deal in a short time, founding tenants' groups, obtaining much hidden information from reluctant council officials, stimulating many local people. They have unearthed much latent dissatisfaction, and instructed groups as to how they can attempt to rectify wrongs. Most of them, as is the case in almost all new fields, have been employed by voluntary agencies, and most of them have lived in the areas in which they were working. Although democratic and non-directive in theory, in practice they are more knowledgeable than the groups they lead. There is a constant danger of giving a strong lead, of becoming the organizing force and of creating dependency. This is a peril of all professions, but community workers, unlike the clergy, are not invited into the areas at the request of a local group, nor are they paid by or responsible to the groups they serve. All good community workers can recognize and counteract such disadvantages, but in general the voluntary community workers are more successful than the statutory workers. The latter, because they are paid directly by the local government authorities, have an awkward conflict of loyalties between their paymasters and the local groups who are often engaged in bitter battles with the local council. Many of the statutory community workers have been cowed by their political bosses and often stay in one area only for very short periods of time, causing the groups they created to founder.

The most ambitious of the community-work approaches have been the Community Development Projects set up by the Home Office in a dozen different areas in Britain. These were founded and financed under the Urban Aid Scheme to research and initiate social action projects in socially deprived areas. They have had considerable resources of money, partly from the Home Office and partly from the local council of the areas in which they operate. Yet their problems have been many and the approaches and results mixed. In Liverpool they have funded a local newspaper, encouraged new political groupings to run for office, helped the free schools, and worked for local independence in a very desperate local environment. In Coventry they have provided skills and resources not otherwise available. They have tried to persuade the council to provide for what they have interpreted as the needs of the community. In Glamorgan they have helped problem families, and tried to identify transport and employment needs. In Southwark they ran into constant rivalry with their local politicians and local government officers and achieved little. In most of the projects the coalition between the action team and the research team was fragile and often completely disintegrated.

Despite the wide variety of professional helping agencies in the inner-city, certain conclusions are obvious. There is a lack of co-operation between different professional groups, a loss of contact with inner-city problems caused by statutory centralization, an absence of consultation between the agencies and their clients, and a tendency to create rather than relieve dependency. Furthermore, there are disadvantages due to the number of non-resident professional workers, and advantages which voluntary agencies possess compared to their statutory counterparts.

A whole combination of factors is necessary to improve the situation radically in the urban ghettos. There must be a combined, coherent and unified attack on the problems by all the helping agencies. Isolated teachers, politicians and social workers have given new hope to people in despair, ameliorated severe problems and suggested solutions. Working together they can begin to transform the position. There must be a determined attempt to halt professionalization when this has meant excluding the amateurs and the volunteer. It is through a shortage of money and personnel that churches and voluntary agencies have not become isolated elites. There must be a recognition that the problem cannot be solved from the outside. The people must be helped to organize themselves so that they can work to change their condition. Social planning must be controlled from below as well as from above. Local people must be given a chance to plan their own lives and environment. More professional workers must be encouraged and helped to live in the areas in which they work. This will enlarge their perceptions, and give them a real stake in stimulating change. Goodwill and enthusiasm are not enough to change the urban ghetto. There must also be indignation. There must be emotional rebellion coupled with rational constructiveness. The overwhelming need of the inner-city is for indigenous leaders. The aim of all professional help from the outside should be to stimulate and not stifle leadership. The overwhelming efforts of the professional help from the inside, from the settlements, churches and other institutions left in the metropolitan centres, should be to bend all their efforts to discover and develop such leaders in their own healthy human communities. The agencies for change must work stealthily and unobtrusively and persistently to transform the urban ghetto. An ancient Chinese proverb says:

> Of a good leader
>   who talks little
> When his work is done
>   his aim fulfilled,
> They will say
>   'We did this ourselves'.

That is how it must be done.

4. Urban Culture

A major theme of this book has been the ignorance of life in the urban ghetto by those who live outside its walls. This results in a lack of sympathy towards its inhabitants on the part of suburban owner-occupiers, and a lack of realism amongst the many professional workers who attempt to ameliorate or transform its environment. Yet the life of urban dwellers is not as easy to identify and evaluate as the statistics about educational achievement or housing densities. Nevertheless, there is a consensus that life is different in the inner-city from life in the suburbs. Books like Heren's *Growing Up Poor* in London and Jasper's *A Hoxton Childhood* etch in a style of life far removed from that of the majority of their readers.

Professional people who live in the inner-city, such as community workers, clergy and the few representatives of other professions, occupy an unusual position. They straddle the growing gap between the home-owners and the urban poor. By training and education they are members of the professional class; by choice they live and work amongst the dwellers of the inner-city. This gives them a favourable opportunity to interpret the culture of one group to the other. Without some such intermediaries life in the inner-city will remain unknown. Misconceptions may prevent change.

Charles Valentine in the introduction of his book *The Culture of Poverty* gives his views of the only way possible to discover the rules which generate and guide behaviour, the values which are not always overtly expressed in everyday life, the entire way of life of a community, which includes their standards of perceiving, predicting, acting and judging. From the time of the earliest anthropologists it has been recognized that prolonged, extensive, direct exposure to the actual conditions of the life which is being studied has been needed to understand a previously unknown culture. This has involved direct observation of social behaviour and participation in community life as well as systematic questioning and discussion with informants. Only by this immersion in group existence has the anthropologist been able to probe thoroughly beneath the surface of a culture and replace superficial impressions with accurate insights. While he knows that he must ultimately remain an alien, the anthropologist has nevertheless striven to combine his outsider's perception with the insider's view of the culture. By this approach he has discovered the inner coherence of an alien or exotic culture with relative independence from the biases of his own cultural background.

Oscar Lewis was one of the first anthropologists who applied these methods of studying distant tribes to observing the poor in cities. He aimed to try to give a voice to people who are rarely heard. He provided an inside view of a style of life which is common to many deprived groups in our society, bridging the gap in communication between the middle classes and the poor. He hoped that this would lead to a more realistic and sympathetic view of the poor and their problems, and would provide a more rational basis for constructive social action.

Anthropologists have slowly been converted to the need to live amongst and share the experiences of the urban poor whom they are studying. A year is regarded as the minimum time in which it is possible to engage in exposure to the culture of the city. Among those who have the greatest opportunity to study and be moulded by urban culture are the clergy who live in their parishes for many years. They are not academic spectators, strangers observing and recording yet with no role to play. There is still a surprisingly high attendance for rites of passage in church. Although only one in twenty of the local population go regularly to an Anglican church, two out of every three go for baptisms and weddings. The local clergy are known by an enormous number of people, and in a recent survey were ranked near the top of people important to the local community, far above social workers, local councillors or the Member of Parliament.

The local clergy learn of the cultural situation in the inner-city by moving among, talking to, listening to, and working with the people amongst whom they live. This is their source book.

49

The clergy work with differing groups that span the spectrum of life in the inner-city. They work with the grossly deprived trying to improve their conditions individually and corporately. They work with those using the church for major ceremonial occasions. They co-operate with other helping agencies. They also, inevitably, spend much of their time working with their congregations by whom they are paid and to whom they are responsible. The congregation is that good cross-section of the local community with whom the clergyman has his first and most vital contacts. With them he shares an identity of viewpoint and many common presuppositions. Unless he can both learn from them and influence them, he has little hope of rapidly influencing and changing the society in which he finds himself.

The congregation of the local church in the inner-city will be small. Going to church is not part of the social or cultural pattern of the urban poor in England. This is not because the inner-city is full of militant atheists, nor because the church and clergy are part of an alien culture. A local survey in Southwark revealed that over nine people out of ten claimed to believe in a personal God. It is because the urban poor rarely belong to formal organizations of any kind. Social patterns tend to be flexible and informal. Long-term commitment is the rarity. One of the elements that gives the culture of poverty its anachronistic and marginal quality is the low level of organization. There is often a higher level of socio-cultural organization amongst primitive peoples than in a fragmented and apathetic city slum. All formal organizations whether they are political parties, parent-teacher associations or churches have low memberships. The work of the clergy is set in a situation of expressed belief but small commitment; of small congregations but considerable respect for the clergy. The church is used for major events. The clergy spend much of their time dealing with people who are sympathetic to the church but who are not members of it.

Large numbers of babies are baptized, although how much of the meaning and obligations of the service penetrate must be doubtful. One Bermondsey church which held its baptisms in the middle of its parish Eucharist had the amusing case of a family, hearing the travelling whelk-stall bell outside the church, sending out a family member to get whelks all round which were then consumed during the rest of the service.

The cultural distinctiveness of the urban poor can be seen easily at the other great rites of marriage and death. Weddings are so deeply embedded in the social fabric of the area that the equation that marriage equals church impels large numbers of couples one or both of whom are divorced to demand a church wedding. There are cultural discontinuities between middle-class and working-class society which are reflected in the weddings. These are more elaborate in the inner-city with anything up to twelve bridesmaids often dressed in different coloured gowns with the odd page boy or two masquerading as a guards officer or a highland chief accompanying the bride. She may be driven to church in a cavalcade of up to three white Rolls-Royces. While the service will be linguistically alien to most of the participants, the hymns mouthed and not sung, and the role of the photographer preceding that of the priest in importance, there is an un-self-conscious vitality about the proceedings, aided by the unfettered presence of myriads of small children, which is both delightful and enviable.

This distinctiveness is equally marked when people die. Few inner-city areas have cemeteries with any space left in them, so the dead often do make the journey that so many attempted and failed to achieve in their lives, the residential journey to a suburban resting-place. Even here, however, they lie not in a tranquil churchyard shrouded by yews but in a huge necropolis, one of fourteen bodies in a grave; for just as the wonders of technology have enabled us to cantilever the urban poor into homes twenty stories in the sky, so it has enabled us to bury them in stacks of coffins descending deeply into the ground. Because the cemeteries are suburban, not many funeral services are held in their local church. Yet death is marked in the urban ghetto with a ritualized and elaborate solemnity. It is never treated informally or casually. Prayers are often said over the dead body whether lying at home or in the undertaker's chapel. Farewells to the dead body often include embraces from the whole family. The cortège is elaborated with extravagant floral tributes – one of the great pop art forms of urban life – and sometimes includes a tour of the dead man's favourite haunts. The mourners are nearly always dressed in black, and the grief at the funeral is open, visible, and often audible. 'Don't let him burn!' screamed one distraught widow at the crematorium committal above the surrounding wails. Despite such extreme manifestations, the open and visible grief is a much more effective way of cauterizing the pain of separation than the fearful stifling of emotion that is the characteristic response of the middle classes to grief and death.

The clergy and other resident professionals work a great deal with young people and their families. Such work can range from helping teachers and parents find suitable schools for the children to helping when sexual assaults have occurred, or being called out to help the mentally ill or suicidal parent. The doorbell may ring late one night to admit a local teacher in the throes of a nervous breakdown. Another evening it will be a woman who has fled from her flat leaving behind the five young children and her husband who has tried to stab her with a carving knife after taking an overdose of drugs. Such insights into the patterns of life in the inner-city come less frequently to those who live outside its boundaries.

Few cultural differences are more noticeable in poor areas than the family structure and the behaviour of children. More families are in the care of one parent. Even when a father is still resident with the family he is often not the strong or dominant influence on the household. He will rarely attend school functions held in the evenings, and will often leave the child-rearing almost entirely to the mother. The children spend less time in the home than in suburban areas often because the small and inadequate home can offer them little. Instead they spend much of their time playing in the streets and on pavements with gangs of friends, as there is nowhere else to play. They often cause considerable annoyance to other residents. The hostility between young and old is an important element in the inner-city. One pensioner was so terrified by the local children climbing on to the roof of her old person's bungalow, by their banging on her windows and stuffing dead rats through her letter box, that she often spent the nights on the central railway stations for peace. She sneaked out of her bungalow in the evenings, returning at daybreak. Discipline in many families is arbitrary and sporadic, varying from indulgence one day to being chased down the street the next by a father yelling, 'I'll kill you when I catch you!' In many homes children lack guidance. More seriously, they lack a steady demonstrative affection and a knowledge that they are loved and accepted.

Violence is one of the most destructive elements in working-class culture. It can erupt during festivities as well as in situations of conflict and challenge. A wedding reception which, unlike middle-class affairs, almost always involves substantial portions of food, a full-scale dance and large quantities of alcohol, is a common occasion for violence. In one instance it all started from a long-standing family feud. One young man thought another had insulted his wife. He made a fuss. The other flared up. Some pushing and shoving and the whole erupted into a running fight that pulsed down the church-hall steps, into the street, the mêlée growing as other relatives and friends joined in. The men alternately were swinging punches and trying to separate the original combatants, the women screaming obscenities. The noise level rose. All the inhabitants of the flats around the square leaned out of their windows. Half of them enjoyed the free entertainment, the other half protested at having been woken up at midnight. The bride departed in tears, complaining with some justification that her wedding day was ruined. Eventually the fighting died down and the police arrived. The parents tried to calm the terrified and exhausted young children. One little girl of three kept crying, 'My daddy has been killed, my daddy has been killed.'

At another wedding reception a gun was produced and used for threatening guests after the money for the wedding photographs had been stolen. A general fight broke out. The bride got knocked down in all her white finery. One brawler turning to another asked, 'What are you hitting me for, I'm your brother?' At a third reception everyone was peacefully dancing except the bride's father and the groom's father who were having a fight in the middle of the dance floor.

It is scarcely surprising that with such examples the age of children's getting involved in serious affrays drops constantly. Thirteen-year-old boys break bottles and throw chairs in local dances, and one local fourteen-year-old was on remand for assaulting an old lady who was taken to hospital needing forty stitches in her head. The children are fiercer, more destructive and fight harder because of their restricted horizons. Violence is the typical reaction of the inarticulate. These are some of the negative aspects of working-class culture which are seen and suffered by all who live in the urban ghetto. There are those who assert that there are no other aspects. They claim that the urban ghetto consists of the alienated, ignorant and apathetic who see their lives as devoid of success or satisfaction. They maintain that the ghetto is distinguished by low levels of expectation and aspiration, by disorganization and a lack of social control and community organizations. The inner-city is characterized by resignation, fatalism and a lack of purposeful action. The culture of poverty is recognizable by the poverty of its culture.

It would be a tragedy if the culture of the urban ghetto were entirely negative, not just because of the misery of its inhabitants' lives, but also because of the lack of motivation which would stem from such despair. A deteriorating family structure leads to poor education, to crime and social violence and to the cycle of poverty. If the major cause of the plight of the poor and despised is the internal deficiency of their own way of life then it is difficult to see how this cause can be remedied.

Such a picture is far from the truth. It is distorted by the very fact that so many observers of the poor are biased by their class presuppositions. It is not the fault of the poor that they are poor. They are the dispossessed of an unjust society. The characteristic reaction to the inhabitants of the inner-city is mingled fear and contempt. Observations about the culture of the urban ghetto should not spring from fear or contempt but from unsentimental compassion. The culture of the inner-city is based on poverty and deprivation. The essence of poverty is inequality – of wealth, occupations, education and political power.

The problem is that the cultural strengths are less overt than the weaknesses. Just as the bare facts fail to reveal the human anguish and sense of powerlessness that pervade the inner-city areas, so facts can do little to emphasize the cultural strengths. All that can be done is to dot in a few indications and hope that, like a pointillist painting, a picture looms out of the stipples.

The language of the inner-city lacks finesse, but not vigour. From rhyming slang to the patter of the barrow boys it has a cutting edge blunted elsewhere. There is a generosity, a willingness to help with time and skills, which is lacking in more individualistic areas. There is a community flavour, a spirit which eliminates the pallid isolation of the suburbs. There is a vigour and self-confidence about the decorative arts, about clothes and fashions and home ornamentation. There is an immense capacity for hard work. Many men and women hold down two jobs simultaneously. There is a love of trading, buying and selling, wheeling and dealing. Street markets are an ineradicable part of the inner-city panorama. There is the tremendous resilience in the face of hardship and disaster whether it emanates from natural disasters or the slings and arrows of outrageous authorities.

It is easy to be pessimistic about the inner-city, its environment and culture, to assume that every aspect of the urban ghetto is fast deteriorating. Yet there is evidence of cultural progress.

There have been several references to violence in this chapter but the evidence is that this has declined rather than increased. There are fewer brawls outside public houses than in the past. Few husbands hit their wives, nor would such an assault be accepted as part of the natural order as it was in their grandparents' day. There may still be occasional violent behaviour at weddings, but there used to be far worse outbreaks at funerals. Police were once called upon to stand duty at gravesides to prevent family brawls. Coachloads of mourners piled out of their hired transport to battle it out on their way to the cemetery. There is less condonation of violence. The man whose neighbour was having her head smashed against his front door by the man upstairs (to whom she had complained about the noise from his children) opened his door to request mildly, 'Please do you mind not making so much noise' and shut the door. He is now atypical.

Clergy and other resident professionals in the inner-city see the cultural distinctiveness not only of individuals but also of groups. These are informal and it is not easy to hold groups together, for committee skills are lacking and conflicts of

55

virulent intensity occur often. Whether the groups are of tenants, or school-parents or church goers there is the conflict between established beliefs and challenging ideas. Yet while the formation and maintenance of strong groups are difficult, the persecution of the urban poor has resulted in social cohesiveness and communal values surviving their demise in other areas. There is less stress on individual power and personal possession. Those who live in the inner-city have to test their observations and interpretations against the background of the individuals and groups among whom they live and work.

Britain remains divided into classes and areas. Too many workers live in specially constructed enclaves, the council estates. These are conveniently situated near the worst schools. Working-class children know almost from their first moment of consciousness that most of them are probably destined to follow the footsteps of their fathers, into manual or skilled-hand labour. They have far less chance, proportionate to their numbers, of entering university than upper-class children. For all but a few, outstanding jobs in the city or top positions in industry or the professions are not worth even dreaming about. A bank account is the exception rather than the rule. Taxis are driven not ridden in. Medical treatment is a matter of long queues and frustrating delays. There is nobody to influence when complaints against companies or higher authorities have to be made. Workers read different newspapers, shop in different shops, eat different foods, and take absolutely different holidays from those on the upper levels of society. Individual freedom exists in proportion to wealth. A rich man is free to do much as he pleases – to take quarrels to court, to live abroad, to intimidate suppliers, to buy private medical treatment or excellent education for his children. A poor man can do none of these. Although the workers have grown richer along with the rest of society, they have only slightly closed the gap between themselves and the higher-income groups.

This enormous gap between the life style, wealth and culture of those in the urban ghetto and those outside is a main cause of Britain's economic stagnation and condemns huge numbers of people to poverty and misery. The cultural distinctiveness between those in the inner-city and those outside it exacerbates the conflicts between the two groups and vitiates the culture of both.

The only way that such cultural and economic gaps can be closed is by individuals and institutions which exist both in and outside the urban ghetto. This can include resident social workers and teachers as well as the outposts of schools and universities whose settlements remain numerous in the inner-city. Above all it must mean the church and its clergy. Existing as it does both in the inner-city and in the suburbs the church is in a strong position to understand and interpret the two cultures to each other. There is no certainty that the church will succeed in leading a movement to destroy the walls of the ghetto. It has been reluctant to attempt this in the past, and unsuccessful when it has tried; but given the will to work and the courage to attempt the task it is in the best position to bridge the cultural ravine that separates the urban ghetto from those outside its walls.

5. Rebuilding the Church

In May, 1968, the Rev. Douglas Bartles-Smith was instituted as parish priest of St. Michael and All Angels and All Souls with Emmanuel, Camberwell, by Bishop John Robinson. As indicated by its lengthy title the parish was the result of a recent amalgamation of three parishes. This amalgamation resulted in twenty parishioners worshipping in a decaying Victorian building which could seat six hundred people. The situation was so desperate that the remaining parishioners were prepared for any experiment, any challenge.

They rapidly agreed to two major decisions. The first was to establish links with the neighbouring church of St. Paul, Newington. The second was to move from their church. Upon the development of these two decisions hung the ability of the church in the area to play a major role in revitalizing the religious life and community development of the area.

The parochial system has many strengths, including being rooted in the realities of the local situation. It has corresponding weaknesses, especially in the inner-city. St. Paul's and St. Michael's were both sited in a decaying area which was being comprehensively redeveloped into a huge new housing estate, the Brandon Estate. This was started in the late fifties and will not be completed until the early eighties. The parochial boundaries split the estate. The parishes showed no corresponding identity with the rebuilt communities. Separate parishes breed isolation among clergy and congregations. They create fear and suspicion of outsiders. They prevent shared use of valuable resources. Consequently there has been a search for new structures which maintain the strengths of the parochial system while overcoming its weaknesses.

The two major alternatives are team ministries and group ministries. A team ministry is the combining of several parishes into one new parish. It is led by one rector who presides over a team of clergy some of whom are attached to the previous parish churches. A group ministry is a close working relationship between separate parishes which maintain their separate vicars, churches and parish councils, and finances. In both cases there are many different ways of organizing and working the new structure. (See diagram on page 60 for our solutions.)

Douglas Bartles-Smith and the Parochial Church Council of St. Michael's approached the parish of St. Paul's to explore together the possibility of future links. The first joint decision was to combine together to start a church-sponsored community newspaper *Compass*, replacing the previous parish newspaper produced solely by St. Paul's. *Compass* began in the autumn of 1968. The second decision was to found an informal group of laity and clergy from the two parishes to investigate the possibilities of a group or team ministry. This originated in the summer of 1968. From the beginning it included other Christians working in the area. Members included a Roman Catholic Educational Welfare Officer, a Methodist minister, the headmaster of St. Michael's School, and an educational psychologist.

In the autumn of 1968 the vicar at St. Paul's, Newington resigned. The group wrote to the Bishop of Southwark urging him to appoint a new priest who would be sympathetic to the idea of links with St. Michael's. The Bishop appointed the Rev. David Gerrard who was inducted as the vicar of St. Paul's in March, 1969. He arrived at a church which had been rebuilt after its destruction through bombing in the war. It was rebuilt on a lavish scale with a church, a hall, and a purpose-built youth centre. These premises needed a great deal of maintenance and were a considerable strain on the time and finances of a congregation decimated by considerable parochial redevelopment.

With the new parish priests at both St. Michael's and St. Paul's, both parishes began to debate the best form of parochial reorganization. By the autumn of 1969 it was clear that the overwhelming number of parishioners were in favour of a group ministry. Both Parochial Church Councils ratified this choice with only two members at St. Paul's voting against this decision. It was two years before the legal formalities were

WORKINGS OF THE GROUP COUNCIL

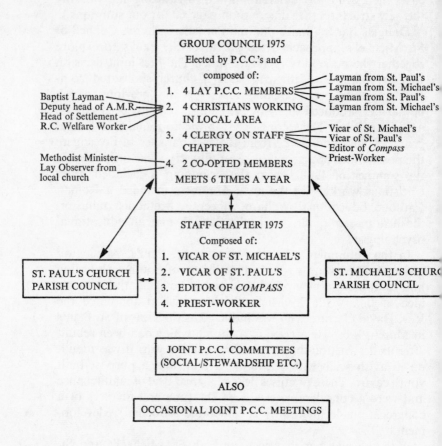

*ALL GROUP-MINISTRY DECISIONS MUST BE AGREED BY
BOTH PAROCHIAL COUNCILS*

completed, but effectively the group ministry began in September, 1969.

Group ministry meant that the two parishes bound themselves to work together in a federation. The clergy met for a staff meeting every week. A Group Council was formed with two lay members elected by both Parochial Church Councils and four other Christians also elected jointly by the two Councils. This enabled other Christians who worked in the area to contribute their help and advice. Later a joint social committee was established to run all the social activities, and a joint stewardship committee to run the stewardship campaigns. All joint activities had to be approved by the Group Council and by the two Parish Councils.

Group ministry was the deliberate choice of the lay people of both parishes. They understood the enormous advantages that came from linking up with another parish. These included the sharing of resources, the destruction of artificial boundaries, the wider vision, the increased influence on the local community, the help to isolated clergy, and the psychological boost to congregations of doubled attendances at joint functions. Yet they did not wish to lose the local nature of their churches, the identity with the back streets of their area, their limited activities and personal links with local residents. It is these benefits which give the parish churches so many advantages over the far larger structures and organizations of schools, social-work areas or political wards in helping the local community. A team ministry would have meant one vast parish and the loss of an individual vicar who was well known and easy to contact. A group ministry was seen as keeping the local church local, yet enabling it to act effectively over a large housing estate when needed. Another reason the laity far preferred a group to a team ministry was a desire not to be excluded when decisions were made. There is far more lay participation in a group ministry than there can be in a team ministry with its strong centralized team of clergy and with the reduction in powers of the Parochial Church Councils. Many felt a team ministry was a reversion to the Victorian conception of a large parish with several daughter churches run by curates.

The main anxiety of the laity concerned the question of

61

leadership. Most jobs are hierarchical. An order is given from a superior to an inferior and passed on down the line. It was feared that without a clearly designated leader there would be either leadership conflicts or a leadership vacuum. In fact, leadership is far more subtle than is implied by the simple giving and receiving of orders. In a group ministry the vicars exercise individual direction in their own parishes and a corporate leadership in arriving at joint decisions. The formal chairmanship of the group council rotates annually, and is held by laymen as well as clergy.

The main advantage of the group ministry for all the clergy has been the regular weekly staff meeting followed by a staff lunch. In the inner-city it is almost inevitable that an isolated priest surrounded by many problems becomes depressed and apathetic. There is great value to the clergy in a group where difficulties can be recognized and discussed, and solutions proposed. In the summer of 1975 the staff consisted of an educational psychologist, Rev. Terry Clayton, who helped in the evenings and on Sundays, and Rev. Henry Morgan who edited *Compass*, and David Gerrard and Douglas Bartles-Smith.

The establishment of the group ministry in the autumn of 1969 resulted in an immediate boost to both churches. Morale was raised by undertaking new projects which were not possible for separate congregations. New members, most of them young, were attracted into the church. The numbers of church members grew every year, despite the rapidly falling populations of the area as a result of the demolition of old properties. Over the years the combined attendance of the two churches has trebled, and their spirit and enthusiasm has grown. It has not been narrowly confined to the buildings and organizations of the church, but has also resulted in far more activity in the life of the community.

Before detailing the progress made by the group ministry in many fields it is, however, necessary to return to the second great decision made by the people of St. Michael's. This was to leave their large, old church. The decision to move was forced upon them by the unwieldy size of the old building and by the enormous costs needed to restore and maintain it. The old church also suffered from the disadvantage of poor siting. It was isolated from the new estates that had been built in the parish, and consequently it was decided to rebuild the church on a new site. St. Michael's Secondary School was situated centrally in the parish. It was planned to expand it into a seven-form entry comprehensive school by combining it with another church secondary school. After considerable discussions with the school governors, the educational authorities of Southwark Diocese, the Inner London Education Authority and the Department of Education and Science, the Parish Council agreed to build the new church on the expanded site of the new comprehensive school, to be called Archbishop Michael Ramsey School. As the school site was sub-standard – an almost universal disadvantage of inner-city schools – the church would have to be a dual-purpose building used by the school during the week. As the school authorities needed a music centre for the new school, the school architect was commissioned to draw up plans for an easily adaptable building suitable for music teaching, practice rooms and orchestral rehearsals, and also for a centre of worship for the whole parish. Fortunately, the architect had experience of designing both churches and schools, and produced a solution which satisfied both church and school authorities.

The walls of the music centre were covered with pin boards and blackboards for displays and teaching purposes. A raised step and dais at one end of the room formed a visual centre for musical performances. Four small rooms off the centre were practice rooms for instrumentalists. On Sundays and for major evening services the building was easily and rapidly transformed. Curtains were drawn around all four walls, concealing the musical displays. Between one hundred and one hundred and fifty chairs were set out. A collapsible altar was erected from the dais where it lay during the week. Three of the practice rooms became small vestries for clergy, servers and church-wardens. The largest of the rehearsal rooms was used for refreshments and as a licensed bar. The decision to open a bar was agreed by the Parish Council and the school governors. They rightly felt that this facility would enable the building to be used as a centre of community, available to local groups, and not merely for schoolchildren and church people.

63

St. Michael's parish paid the total cost of the church and music centre out of the proceeds of the sale of two redundant churches in its parish. The cost was only £40,000 and this left a residue of £80,000 which was given to the diocese towards building a new church for the huge new Thamesmead estate built on riverside marshland in Erith. The maintenance costs of the new church were shared between St. Michael's Church and the Inner London Education Authority. The Authority pays 80% of all the heating, lighting, cleaning, repair and decoration costs, and the church pays the remaining 20%. Thus the maintenance costs paid by the church are relatively modest. It does not – as many parishes are forced to – spend most of its time and energy on raising money to keep the church open. Just as the school uses the church during the week, so the church has the right to use the rest of the school premises for sunday schools, dances and social events. The final plans for the dual-purpose building were only agreed by the central church authorities because St. Michael's had joined in a group ministry with St. Paul's. All parishioners have the right to be married, buried and baptized from their parish church. As St. Michael's Church was used for educational purposes during the week, this would not have been possible, but by becoming a group ministry all parishioners could on weekdays be married in, or buried from, St. Paul's Church.

The new church and music centre was dedicated in October, 1972 and the new Archbishop Michael Ramsey School opened in September, 1974. The school is a centre of community. Teachers stay behind after school to run clubs and youth activities for the whole neighbourhood. The buildings are used most evenings not only by church and school, but also by the St. John Ambulance Brigade, by tenants' associations and other organizations.

At St. Paul's Church the problems of effective use of the buildings were also intractable. A large modern building with church, hall, and youth centre is difficult and expensive to maintain, and is often under-used. The youth centre and the church hall were let to the Inner London Education Authority for use as an Educational Guidance Centre. Here children with particular behavioural problems and a history of disruptive activity in schools are given intensive care by specially trained teachers. The youth centre is open every evening, and is used for holiday play-schemes during school vacations. The church hall is used for badminton and trampolining by the youth club and also by tenants' groups, play committees and the community development project in the area.

There is often a shortage of available halls for community meetings and activities, and the church is in an excellent position to provide a cheap meeting place for many emergent and established groups and organizations in the area.

Restrictive parochial structures were overcome by the establishment of a group ministry, and the unwieldy church premises were rationalized for the benefit of church and community. However, the church is far more than structures and buildings. The church is the Christian family gathered for worship and sent for service. It is an example to its neighbourhood in the enjoyment of life, and in the endurance of life. The activities of the group ministry show the use made of the new structures and buildings.

The first decision made was that the care both of individual Christians and the church family by the clergy should never be neglected in favour of social or political activism. It is a prevalent temptation for radical priests to concentrate on social casework and community development work while neglecting the worship and teaching of their own Christian congregations. This results in declining, ignorant and apathetic congregations who are unwilling and unable to contribute anything towards helping their local community and towards solving its problems. The church must involve itself in all the difficulties, disadvantages and problems found in the inner-city areas. But these problems will not be solved by clergymen. They will only be affected by lively Christian congregations acting out their Christian beliefs in the situation in which they live.

The central action of the Christian family is to meet together around the Lord's Table, and to worship together in the Eucharist. Through a joint liturgical committee, through involving the laity in readings, intercessions and thanksgiving, through modern musical settings and joint worship on special occasions, the centrality of worship has permeated through both churches.

65

This has resulted in steadily growing congregations during a decade of inner-urban depopulation and nationally declining church attendances. These increases have been regular, but a special effort was made for the opening of the new St. Michael's Church with a mission to the whole area assisted by a mission team from the Church Army.

While increasing numbers are always encouraging no church can be satisfied simply by filling its pews. Many new members of inner-city churches have little religious background, a meagre knowledge of the Bible, a small conception of church doctrines, and little interest or concern in church history. If they are to become effective and committed church members despite the secular pressures to which they are subjected at work and in their general environment, the church has to provide not only significant worship but also a friendly community and effective lay training. The best way of informing church members was in concentrated bursts of activity. Especially helpful have been opportunities to go away for a weekend to study and learn. The first weekends were held at a Diocesan Conference Centre. The weekends were largely concerned with planning for the future and, as the Centre could only accommodate forty people, were largely restricted to members of the parish councils and their families. After widespread demands in September, 1974 one hundred parishioners went for a weekend to Aylesford Priory, in Kent. There were lectures on the Bible, on personal relationships, on the theology of work, and on the nature of the church. There were also study groups, including one for teenagers. Out of the Aylesford experience sprang a demand for more regular and disciplined Bible studies, which were later established. As well as the more concentrated lay-training exercises there were annual joint Lent courses, with speakers varying from Enoch Powell to a local squatters' leader, and subjects varying from politics to prayer.

If one can make such a fragile distinction, opportunities were created not only for Christian learning, but also for spiritual growth. Retreats were regularly held. Joint pilgrimages were arranged to Canterbury and Walsingham. As well as being of immeasurable value to the individuals who took part, all these occasions were indispensable in enabling the people of the two parishes to meet, to mix to share in fellowship, and to become real friends.

One of the characteristics of inner-city life is the love of social events. Churches are wise if they build on the strengths of their environment, and consequently many joint social activities have been organized by the joint social committee. There are several dances every year, with the band and the discotheque being provided by teenage church members. Theatre trips are always popular as are the coach excursions to seaside and country. Every year there is a joint harvest supper for 150 church members, cooked and served by members and their families, and followed by cabaret and dancing. Other social events are organized to celebrate important church festivals. Perhaps the most ambitious social occasion was a parish holiday in July, 1975 when over 150 parishioners took over Lancing College (a private school on the south coast with which St. Michael's Church has historic links) for a weekend of sports, swimming, dancing and barbecues and general relaxation. Such social events are enjoyable yet not trivial. They create community, and they form an easy route for non-Christians to meet and share in the fellowship of a Christian family.

One danger for any close-knit family is exclusiveness. It is only too easy to be so preoccupied with one's own concerns that anyone outside the family is frozen out. The group ministry has tried to avoid this danger in several ways. Through group council membership and by personal contacts it has made approaches to other churches. It initiated events during Christian Unity Week. Services have been held in Orthodox, Methodist, Roman Catholic and Baptist churches in the area, and close co-operation with the clergy and people of other churches has been sought. Another way in which exclusiveness has been avoided has been by welcoming visits and enquiries from other churches about the workings of the group ministry. The clergy have visited several other parishes interested in establishing group ministries, and their comments, queries and criticisms have been invaluable in preventing smugness and self-satisfaction. The group ministry was the first one established in the Southwark diocese and in May, 1975 it presented a display in Southwark Cathedral to all members of the diocesan synod.

Perhaps the most important step in avoiding exclusiveness has been a determination to share out money and time and work with those outside the parishes. Both churches have given more money to missions since the establishment of group ministry than before. Both joined together in May, 1975 for a sponsored fast by the clergy to raise money for Christian Aid, which raised over £160 from church members. Two joint stewardship campaigns have been held, the first in October, 1971, the second in October, 1975. In both of them the need for church members to give generously of their time and energy as well as their money to activities other than the church was stressed. Both resulted not only in more realistic levels of parochial giving, but also in a greater interest in what needed to be done in the wider community. The twin themes which are central to this chapter, and to this whole book, have been the need to build up vigorous Christian churches in the inner-city, and the need for social and political action by the churches in co-operation with other organizations to improve the deprived and desolate state of inner-city life. The churches can only avoid a selfish pietism by being concerned with the total life of the neighbourhood of which they are a vital and integral part. The group ministry avoided excessive parochialism by involving itself and its members in campaigning for radical social change in its area. It could do this effectively because of the vigour and strength of its membership. And its membership grew in numbers and power because it was seen to care for the whole lives of those in its area.

The group ministry arranged open political meetings before borough, Greater London Council, and national elections. Candidates from all parties attended, and after short speeches, many local voters took the opportunity to question their future Member of Parliament or their future councillor. It was the only local opportunity for voters to see, hear and judge the candidates. The large numbers attending such meetings showed how the opportunity was welcomed. The candidates themselves, after original hostility and suspicion, also came to value this exercise in communication.

Another broadening of communication by the group ministry

concerned a very different aid to the community. Owing to the shortage of play-space the holiday period can be a trial to parents and children. For many years a holiday play-scheme was run in St. Michael's school premises by boys from Lancing College. Over one hundred children were taken on excursions, played games, engaged in art during the Easter holidays. This was of benefit not just to the local children, but also to the private schoolboys from a very different social background. These boys joined with girls from a boarding school and with sixth formers from local comprehensive schools in a social studies course organized by the group ministry. The church is in an excellent position to help destroy the walls of ignorance and hostility which surround the urban ghetto.

In the group ministry there was none of the common separation between church members and other local groups. Nor was there the frequent pattern of a priest involved in local affairs to a degree that was resented by his congregation who shared none of his concerns, and who felt that he was neglecting his real work. Individual church members are very active in their community. In the past five years members of the group ministry have chaired two local tenants' associations, been active in six others, run a local adventure playground, worked as play group leaders, and been active in Parent-Teacher Associations. Four members have sat on old people's committees, one has been warden of some old people's flats, and one a local councillor. Several members have been involved in a campaign for more parental involvement in schools, and another is chairman of a local youth club. One of the incidental benefits of the sale of a redundant church in St. Michael's parish to the borough council was an agreement that the church could nominate people working in the area and unable to find accommodation in it for a council flat. These five flats have mostly been filled with teachers working at local schools. These teachers, with the group ministry members who are school managers and governors, have increased the educational involvement of the church.

In the seven years from 1968 to 1975 a reformation transformed three vital areas of the church's work. The establishment of the group ministry provided a flexible structure. This enabled the area to be dealt with in its totality, freed from the artificiality of parochial boundaries. Secondly, the considerable resources available to the church in respect of churches, halls, flats, and school premises were used more effectively to benefit both church and community. Finally, the human resources of congregations which had grown in size, confidence and maturity could be used to play a significant and enlarged role in the neighbourhood. The churches had nurtured their members so that they realized they existed not only to bring people to a belief in God and to worship Him, but also to send people out of the churches to become involved in their local affairs as part of their involvement in the kingdom of God.

6. Compass —
A Community Newspaper

The first major initiative taken by the group ministry was the foundation in 1968 of a community newspaper, *Compass*. It was started after consultations with tenants' groups, social clubs and settlements, but the church was the only local body strong enough to provide the finance, leadership and manpower to sponsor and nurture such a major initiative as a local newspaper. *Compass* provides a forum of expression for local residents, a voice for the voiceless. It combats the apathy that results from a lack of power, from the inability of individuals and groups to influence the decisions which affect their lives.

A major part of the endeavours of *Compass* is to encourage and stimulate local efforts at self-help. Particularly important is the need to band together in order to be heard by those who ignore individuals. The second editorial said,

> Individuals tend to get discouraged when they start something worthwhile and it fails through lack of support. It's easy to give examples in our own community. Apathy is all around us, and even when they are personally threatened, many people will hardly lift a finger to help themselves.

> What is the answer? Mr. Shaw of Carter Street has it. He said the other day, 'We must have a Residents Association, for singly we cannot do anything.' *Compass* supports Mr. Shaw and others who feel the same way.

> There are two good reasons for having Residents Associations. First of all there is strength in numbers when it comes to doing something about putting right injustices, and secondly there's the possible bonus of a happier community when people learn to work together for the common good. This paper is anxious to back this sort of community development to the hilt.

The appearance of articles and photographs about the activities of local tenants' groups, playgroups and parent-teacher associations actively encourages the leaders and

71

members of such groups. When groups are dispirited both by official indifference and also by members' apathy, such publicity is vital to them.

There has been an enormous number of different community groups reported in *Compass*. One consisted entirely of young teenagers who claimed some derelict wasteland as their own, and transformed it into their own adventure playground. In July, 1975 *Compass* featured their activities and printed a picture of their tree house, their rope swings and climbing frame, all built from scavenged materials. The older children organized and built the playground without any adult help, and even provided help and supervision for the younger children on the site. As well as frequent stories about schools and children, contributions by children are often printed. These range from comments about their homes – 'Our flat looks like a prison from the outside, they should make each block a different design' – to poems about Bonfire Night, like this from a nine year-old:

> Fireworks! Fireworks!
> Lots of Sparks
> Show up bright
> In the dark
> There's pushing, shoving and shouting about me
> There are things I see with colours around me.

The inner-city is often depressing, so *Compass* has always tried to print hopeful and encouraging news as well as mirroring the legitimate complaints and grievances. It has tried to report the many heartening activities of local associations, the improvements in opportunities for children's play, and also stories reflecting the resilience and vitality of the inhabitants of South London.

In 1973 a nine-year-old boy was killed by a car while crossing John Ruskin Street. This street was used as a fast short-cut between two main roads despite the fact that it divided a large estate. After the boy's death local parents blocked the street and marched to County Hall to press for a safe crossing point. Despite their actions, and despite the death, the response from the local authority and municipal authority was characteristically slow and cautious. *Compass* printed the story of the initial protests, then of the first success: the erection of some railings separating the pavements from the road. It helped to sustain the campaign, for after the first protests it is easy to sink back into lethargy when no results occur. A newspaper, even a small local one, can have a galvanic effect on local authority employees, especially when stories are repeated in local and national papers, or are reported on radio or featured on television. The due application of pressure through a newspaper was one of the most effective ways in which *Compass* helped to improve the inner-city. By adopting and featuring local issues the paper was able to inform and influence its local readers and those who took decisions concerning them so that ignorance was dispelled and injustices rectified.

Compass is directed by an editorial board. The first members were a local community worker, a teacher, a youth leader and local clergy. It soon became obvious that to maintain continuity and effectively to cover the whole area, an editor was needed. The editor also needed to know all the organizations and leaders in the local community to encourage them to contribute to the paper. Since 1973 the editor has been the Rev. Henry Morgan, and not only have increasing numbers of residents written for the paper, but they have also become members of the editorial board. A tenants' leader, a local policeman and others have helped to make the editorial board one of the few organized structures where residents and professional workers meet as equals. In February, 1976 Henry Morgan was appointed vicar of St. Michael's, and his job as editor passed to the deputy editor Margaret Prosser. She is a local mother who worked in the Information and Advice Centre for the Borough of South-wark and is a member of one of the local churches.

In 1972 *Compass* was sold in St. Mary's parish, and the rector of St. Mary's joined the editorial board. Over 2,500 copies are printed monthly, and the paper is sold to one in three homes in the area, a far higher percentage than is reached by any other local paper.

Originally the paper consisted of four pages of local material with a national inserted section. This was never satisfactory as the national articles and columns were seldom of local interest. So in 1974 the insert was dropped, and an eight-page paper

73

consisting of entirely local news was produced. A year later two more pages were added, written by a group of senior citizens and consisting of news of neighbourhood interest for pensioners. These pages contain much lively material, the most popular section being accounts of past times. There have been accounts of picketing during the General Strike, of celebrating Empire Day at school, and of more personal memories like the following story of a street party seen by the author from an upstairs window when he was a small boy before the first world war.

'My father set up his portable harmonium, neighbours gathered round, and there was the clink of jugs, bottles and glasses. Dad began playing a popular chorus which was taken up at once. But the harmony was shattered by the discordant voice of a policeman who told dad that people were complaining about the noise. Dad shut the lid down and invited the P.C. to have a sociable drink, which he did, and went on his way with lots of friendly good-nights. As soon as he was out of earshot, dad started again. But soon the copper was back! However, he seemed more amiable and accepted another drink and a chair. Dad finished his song and did his party piece, "There's a difference between East and West" which extolled the virtues of the poor as opposed to the vices of the rich.

There came a shuffling and a murmur of voices downstairs in our house which I discovered was the policeman, now asleep, being laid down in our passage. When I came down in the morning I half-expected to see our P.C. still lying in the passage but was told that in the early morning, as they could not wake him up, the men had laid him on a barrow and propped him up inside the entrance to the chemist's opposite the Police Station in the hope that one of his mates would help him. And later I heard from dad that he had been moved to another district.'

Compass is distributed by a band of eighty, most of whom are church members. More *Compasses* can be sold by distributors on a street-to-street basis than through local newsagents' shops. It also enables distributors to build up a friendship with their neighbours to whom they sell the paper, to learn of their problems and to encourage purchasers to write letters and articles for the paper. One wrote:

'Could you help to get Gothic Court cleaned up? I have written to Mr. Goodwin of the Greater London Council, he thinks the cleaning is done, but I am telling the truth when I say they have never put a broom or shovel in our places; the chutes stink as they have never been washed out, and we have maggots in them. Also we have two holes on the green where the children dig, make mud pies and throw them at the windows. I have spoken to the caretakers; they stand and grin but do nothing about it.'

The publishing of such letters not only informs others of the problem and relieves the mind of the writer, but it also encourages reform of abuses – especially when a copy of the paper is forwarded to the relevant department of the local authority. Such positive results encourage many local people who have never previously written any letter for publication to write to the paper. *Compass* publishes all letters it receives. People respond with increasing frequency, and express themselves with more and growing confidence.

One of the most important roles of *Compass* is as a campaigning paper, spotlighting the abuses and the omissions of power as they affect the neighbourhood. The chief target for local criticism has been the council, both its elected members and its paid officials. Because Southwark has had one-party rule for over half a century, the Labour Party has a monopoly of political decision. The major decisions are taken in the secret party caucus. In 1975, when there was a vote in Council Meeting, one member did not know how to vote! People become cynical and apathetic about politics. *Compass* has published many articles and letters bitterly critical of the local council. At elections letters were printed revealing the mockery of the selection of political candidates. A letter in 1971 said:

'The present state of affairs is nothing short of deplorable. The fact of the matter is that in one ward at least of this borough prospective councillors are nominated by a mere handful of votes. In one case it appeared that the numbers of votes cast exceeded that of those eligible to vote.'

Three years later another letter was published on the same theme:

'In my ward the candidates were not adopted solely on the

75

votes of the local members of the party. The Labour Party Constitution allows officers of the Constituency Party to attend, vote and question candidates at the ward selection conferences. They are influential in this process. This means that people not living in a particular ward can vote for or against those wishing to be adopted. This peculiar position is made worse when the ward party is not well attended. In my ward tenants' leaders who were hoping to be adopted came under very heavy fire from the roving party secretary and chairman whereas other prospective candidates did not. Does this occur in other wards too? Is this hostility towards tenants' leaders because of the position they hold or because they are not considered suitable candidates individually by their party officers?'

In 1975 *Compass* antagonized local politicians by revealing that the average attendance at one ward's monthly meetings had sunk to four.

Compass kept as wary an eye on the local Member of Parliament as on the local councillors. It revealed in 1971 that he had only voted in 60 divisions out of a possible 480. He had neglected constituency duties to pursue business interests. These charges, which were reprinted by the local papers and the *Sunday Times*, were denied by the Member's agent who called them 'highly regrettable'. A few months later the Member resigned, and his agent then said, 'He should have had the courage to resign earlier.'

As a small, penniless paper *Compass* was immune from prosecution for libel, so it was free to print material shunned by other papers. In 1971 there was a local squatting campaign against Southwark Council which would not allow its thousand empty homes to be used for temporary accommodation for the homeless. *Compass* supported the squatters' proposals to restrict squatting to Southwark's homeless families, and to undertake repairs and vacate the properties when they were due for redevelopment. It also published photographic evidence that the council's workmen were destroying homes to prevent squatters using them. Partially as a result of these revelations and of continuing publicity, the council eventually reached a compromise with the squatters, allowing the use of unwanted council homes by homeless families.

Another important story first published by *Compass* and then reprinted by other papers was about local residents in Fleming Road being in such despair over their housing conditions that they set fire to their own homes. The front-page article was written anonymously by a local social worker who felt it was the only way to focus public attention on the problem. She wrote:

'Fleming Road is one of the many streets in the area which is suffering at the hands of confused and inhuman authority. Through events completely beyond the control of the people who live there, Fleming Road is now flanked by shining new Council houses one side and derelict empty houses on the other. In between and beside a rubbish dump are a row of small terraced houses, much too small for some of the families who live in them. If the people who live in the road could afford all it would take to stop the damp and decay and make their places decent to live in, they would not be living there. There is no hope of getting a transfer, for who would move in if they moved out? Rats scurrying along the road is not part of the scenery most people want! In these conditions is it surprising that friction and hate develop between the residents and the housing authorities, the police and the whole red tape system? Why aren't the authorities making the position clear? Why are there so many different stories about what will happen to Fleming Road? Some people in the area have set fire to their own homes. They weren't mad, they were desperate.'

The printing of the Fleming Road story was not only part of a campaign to improve living conditions, it was also a way of informing its readers about life in their area. *Compass* provides an information service for the community. Some of its contents were about major scandals. Others were less sensational. Maps and plans were printed about areas due for redevelopment. Council decisions were reported. The times and places of councillors' surgeries were given, so readers could approach local councillors with their problems. Articles on how to claim welfare rights were included, as well as advance notice of meetings and social events planned by local organizations.

By providing such information *Compass* has tried to stimulate and educate its readers. It has not been content merely to reflect local opinions. Strong prejudices existed against isolated groups.

The following letter mirrored the feelings of most local residents about the meths drinkers and alcoholics who occupy many public benches on streets, parks and estates:

'These poor creatures are for the most part able-bodied youngish men and women quite capable of leading a normal life, but who do not consider themselves eligible for hard, honest work. So how to treat them? May I offer a suggestion? Open up some out-door detention camps. Supervised by some good old-fashioned sergeant-majors and make the lazy perishers WORK and WORK and WORK until they ACHE and ACHE and ACHE.'

To balance such ignorance, *Compass* publicized an information fortnight on alcoholism under the title, "Meths Drinkers and Drunks – a Local Problem?". Members of the *Compass* board in co-operation with churches, tenants' associations and the local Council on Alcoholism had helped to arrange the information fortnight, the highlight of which was an open meeting at which cured alcoholics explained some of the facts about alcoholism.

Another issue which generated strong feelings was the increasing number of immigrants living in the area. An editorial said, 'There have been disturbing signs recently of the activities of a few bigoted racialists in the area. Two huge slogans were painted on walls near Carter Street saying, "No more niggers in Carter Street". Who are these anonymous cranks with their paint pots? Do they live in the streets they deface or do they come from outside?'

Compass also supported any local initiatives that reduced racial tensions. At Christmas, 1973 the editorial praised a local tenants' association which had donated some of its scarce funds to the appeal for the starving people of Ethiopia. The most serious threat to harmonious relations occurred in 1970 when the South African cricket team was to play a test match at Kennington Oval which is situated close to the *Compass* area. Many community leaders believed that if the match were played, there would have been violent clashes between militant black power groups and the National Front and its supporters. The headmaster of St. Michael's School led other local headmasters in emphasizing that their multi-racial schools would for the first time be seriously affected by racial disturbances if the match were played. *Compass* strongly supported the headmaster, and Bishop David Sheppard, and other local Christians who planned peaceful demonstrations at the Oval. The Secretary of the Surrey County Cricket Club was informed, at a meeting, of the strong local objections to the match's being played especially in regard to exacerbating racial tension in the area. It seems probable that the protests of moderates led by David Sheppard had at least as much influence on cancelling the tour as the more flamboyant activities of Peter Hain and his supporters.

One member of the editorial board is the local home beat policeman, Police Constable Harry Cole. He has provided many contributions to *Compass*, informing readers of life in the neighbourhood. The most dramatic was the story of victimization of an old man by a gang of teenagers. Harry Cole wrote, 'When Mr. Burrows arrived at Molesworth House a little over a year ago, it seemed an ideal move. He was, however, unaware of one thing. He was unaware of the mindless habits of the groups of teenagers who see a poor seventy-year-old as a test of their sick minds. Mr. Burrows slowly received the treatment. Firstly his doors and windows were smashed. Subsequently they were smashed again. In fact they were smashed so many times that they became permanently boarded up. One by one each segment of window was replaced by wood until Mr. Burrows was nailed inside like a rat. Eventually the interior of his home was smashed. A hammer through his television, through his china and his furniture and all we have left is Mr. Burrows himself. It is extremely doubtful if any of these young thugs are capable of even reading so it is not at them that this story is aimed. It is aimed perhaps at you. Are you a parent? Just what do you know know about your children's whereabouts? Could it be your pride and joy who is trying to ruin the last days of an old gentleman when they should be moved by pity? Children have been mischievous to the elderly since the origins of time, but rarely have they shown such vindictive hate. Remember the bell is not tolling simply for Mr. Burrows, it is also tolling for you.'

It would not be surprising if some of the attacks on Mr. Burrows came during the day. Truants from school cause much of the vandalism and petty crime in the inner-city. The Inner London Education Authority tries to fight truancy by means of its Educational Welfare Service, but the Service seems to lack the ability and determination to reduce truancy. *Compass* published an article on truancy, and drew attention to the lack of success in meeting it. 'The Educational Welfare Service may have been increased in numbers, with higher pay, more training, greater efficiency and more responsibilities, but has it reduced the truancy figures?'

Because *Compass* was started by the churches who continued to support and sponsor it, there was always the chance that it would be viewed as church propaganda. To counter this, letters and articles critical of the church were published. The one that obtained the most publicity was in 1975, when *Compass* attacked the Diocese of Southwark and the Church Commissioners for their proposal to purchase a large, £40,000 house in Blackheath for the new Bishop of Woolwich. *Compass* argued that the new Bishop's House ought to be of modest size, cheap and situated in the inner-city. The proposed Bishop's House was rejected.

Compass has frequently been accused of sensationalism, of libel, of a lack of balance, of an absence of charity. It has also often been congratulated on its candour and courage in printing hidden stories. Its policy has been deliberately provocative, to stimulate its readers into thinking about many important current issues. By its brashness it has often succeeded in bringing about changes and improvements in the lives of the local community. *Compass* has been one of the most effective single agents for change in the local community.

7. Community Development

The harsh complexity of inner-city problems dictates that radical improvements must emerge from a combination of internal endeavours and external resources. By far the most hopeful current development lies in community work, when a body of professional people consciously attempt to use their skills to enhance the power, competence and morale of the inhabitants of the urban ghetto.

Community workers try to involve local people in working out solutions to their own needs. The workers attempt to mobilize and utilize the hidden human resources in the community. These rediscovered abilities can transform, through appropriate social action, the environment of the inner-city, and reduce the dependency of the inhabitants on the statutory welfare services.

Much work in the inner-city has been accomplished by individuals and groups who have seen gaps in existing services. They have worked to close the gaps and to co-ordinate the services more closely. There was little consultation or active involvement with the recipients of these services, whether parents, tenants, hospital patients or children. Many welfare provisions have been created and sustained by articulate suburban reformers. The consolidation and implementation of welfare provisions have recently been the almost exclusive preserve of professional workers in the social services, education, health services, planning and housing fields. The urban poor, the principal beneficiaries of such services, have had their contribution limited to their union or political party. They have grown to accept the services as the rights of an urban and industrial society.

Yet the mere provision of increased services, while it has moderated some of the extreme hardships of the urban poor, has hardly affected their general standing. Because the urban

81

poor have seen their situation remain stationary when compared with other groups in society, their dissatisfaction has grown. They have become increasingly disenchanted with the traditional democratic procedures and structures. The mere provision of a vote has been seen to change little. Coupled with the discontent with the small power of a vote is the more subtle disillusionment with the power and ability of professional workers to provide services which are relevant to people and which will radically change their lives. Existing social-work agencies and their professional workers are seen to have failed to make any deep impression upon urban problems. To take but a single example: social case workers are observed working with deprived and inadequate families while ignoring the acute social, economic and environmental conditions which largely cause the problems faced by individual families. The needs of the family were caused by the ills of the area. The redress of needs depends on the cure of the ills.

In the early 1960's there began to be practised in England a form of work known as community development. It flowered most profusely on local authority housing estates. One of its earliest and abiding aims was to give tenants a choice about the conditions in their new housing situation. It soon spread to the old decaying city-centres. It became a rapidly growing field because many social workers, planners and youth workers saw community development as a possible solution to their dissatisfactions with democracy and the welfare state. Consultation and participation were adopted as a way of giving back to the voting citizen some of the power which had been wrested from him by elected representatives, civil servants and professional workers.

Community work explored the ways in which citizens could contribute to decisions which were being made in their name. As such it had relevance to many professional fields of activity. Community work began in underdeveloped countries, especially in East Africa, because it was accepted that the difficulties were so immense that without the education and co-operation of the citizens, without involving them in seeking why change was necessary and how it could be brought about, the massive social and economic problems were insoluble. Community work spread to England with the belated realization that inner-city problems were also so severe that they could not be solved unless their inhabitants were given the opportunity to identify their own needs. Professionals in many fields must become aware of ways in which they can encourage clients to contribute to decisions which affect them. They ought to encourage participation, to add a community work element to their present work.

There are also specialized community workers who encourage people in one particular neighbourhood to participate in all decisions which affect them. Community workers attempt to combat the pervasive miasma of apathy which broods over the inner-city. While suburban protest quickly emerges to combat the threat of an airport, motorway or other species of environmental blight, the urban poor are more likely to react with a weary hopeless shrug, an implicit if unstated belief that nothing can be done. Until community workers, clergy, local teachers, doctors, councillors and tenants' leaders can persuade the urban poor that by combining together they can achieve results which will benefit their environment, nothing can be achieved.

Community work deals with people in a small local community. The rest of this chapter will concentrate on the efforts which have been made in one small area to revitalize the people living there, to give them pride in their own abilities and achievements, and hope for their own future. It is a description of progress by minute particulars, but its relevance is universal.

The first example describes attempts to reform the situation found in a redevelopment area, and shows much of the anguish, despair, ignorance and confusion so often encountered in redevelopment. A letter to *Compass* in April, 1969 was written by a lorry driver living in Beresford Buildings in John Ruskin Street. He wrote:

'Finally after ten years of living in a slum, my family and I are to be rehoused. From the beginning when I moved into Beresford Buildings I was grateful for a roof over our heads, but I thought our situation would be short-lived and that the "great powers that be" would give me somewhere decent to live. I found that no one was interested in the rats, water pouring through the roof, the bugs and the fact that four families were using one toilet and sink for water. Nor that tramps slept on the landings; there was filth beyond belief where the dustbins were stored in the yards; that there was gas lighting and damp walls. My first target to get something done about the disgusting conditions was the private owners who never came round, and the agent, who was completely deaf to all complaints. Then I tried the Local Council, but they were not interested; and then the Sanitary Department Officer, who actually told me to emigrate. All this took months and months and nothing was done. I then decided to take some photographs of the premises and sent letters of protest to the Prime Minister, enclosing the photographs. The Minister of Housing wrote back saying he could not interfere with Local Government or the Greater London Council; the Minister of Health gave the same answer. As regards the sanitary conditions Mr. Heath wrote back saying that he would make enquiries. Mr. Gunter, our local M.P., did not even acknowledge my letter. After all this I was still determined to have a go and wrote again to Mr. Desmond Plummer, leader of the Greater London Council, sending him the photos. He replied in very great detail, and promised some action within a couple of weeks. True to his word a housing representative came to see us, and now we are being rehoused, a total of fifteen families. Once again I must give my deep thanks to Mr. D. Plummer and Mr. Heath. By the way – I voted Labour. I am not a Conservative, but I am thanking those who helped me. Those did not include my local Labour Council or my local Labour M.P.'

Soon after this letter was written to *Compass*, Beresford Buildings was emptied and demolished. The letter-writer had achieved success by his individual persistence and concern in publicizing his appalling housing conditions. He was also aided by the existence of a local community newspaper which could help in publicizing his fight and, by reporting his eventual triumph, encourage others to make similar efforts. It was a striking example of what individual persistence can achieve. Much more typical was the case of Mrs. Seymour, who also lived in John Ruskin Street, only a hundred yards from the victorious lorry driver. Mrs. Seymour's husband had an ulcer; she had bronchitis. They both wanted to leave London and so in 1964 decided to sell their small sweet shop above which they lived. They had been there for twenty years, and looked forward to beginning again on the south coast in a climate more congenial to their health. They found another shop in Bournemouth, bought that, and obtained a buyer for their own shop. When the South London Press announced the area was scheduled for redevelopment, their buyer withdrew. However, they were told that their shop would be compulsorily purchased by the Greater London Council in 1965. So in the September of 1965 Mr. Seymour moved down to their new shop in Bournemouth while Mrs. Seymour stayed behind to protect their old property. It was the first separation of their married lives. They hoped it would only be for a few weeks, but it lasted for over three years. Mrs. Seymour saw her husband and family only on holidays. Her health deteriorated. Three different people dealt with her case at County Hall. One suggested that she simply close down the shop and abandon it, but as she replied, 'You've got to carry on, it's your living.' Eventually Mrs. Seymour's house was compulsorily purchased by the Greater London Council, and she was able to join her husband and family on the south coast.

Her case was typical of many in redevelopment areas in North Southwark in the late sixties and early seventies. On her own, lacking the dramatic case and forceful advocacy of her lorry-driver neighbour, she could merely hope for action to be taken. Sluggardly local-government officers can be forced to act by means of sustained and relentless pressure by many people. They cannot ignore the coercion of a whole street nearly as easily as that of a single individual or family. Two local organizations were attempting to weld people together into effective groups to combat apathy and speed redevelopment. One was the group ministry churches. The other was the local university settlement, Cambridge House. These two organizations, and paramountly the vicar of St. Michaels, Douglas Bartles-Smith, and the Cambridge House community worker, Gerry Williams helped to found many Tenants' and Residents' Associations in areas of old housing stock, redevelopment areas, and on new local-authority estates. Many of the groups achieved far more than lone individual efforts. John Ruskin

Street was one of the few areas where they failed to establish such a grouping. Mrs. Seymour's long wait was the partial result.

In Avenue, Cadogan and Beaconsfield Mansions in Bethwin Road a Tenants' Association was formed. An account of their atrocious housing conditions was published in *Compass* and the South London Press. Resulting from this the television programme *Nationwide* filmed their homes. Yet despite their flair for obtaining favourable publicity, their problems remained. Southwark Council issued a Compulsory Purchase Order. There was a public enquiry and the Compulsory Purchase Order was upheld. The landlord appealed on the grounds that he had been out of the country for the public enquiry and requested a further public enquiry so that his objections could be heard. The tortuous legal steps necessary for councils to obtain Compulsory Purchase Orders give private landlords totally unnecessary scope to delay the order and thus postpone their tenants' rehousing. In this case the tenants had tried publicity without being rehoused. They had persuaded the local council to take out a Compulsory Purchase Order, but they still faced the unenviable prospect of another winter in their homes with essential repairs being indefinitely postponed. So they agreed on a rent strike, withholding all payments until vital repairs were completed. Simultaneously they wrote to the Ministry of Housing, protesting about irregular delays in the granting of a definitive decision about the Compulsory Purchase Order. By Christmas they were rehoused. Without a united effort they would have had to wait much longer. In many examples throughout this local area it was the groups working together who were rehoused far faster than the isolated inhabitants of John Ruskin Street, who rejected the opportunity for corporate action.

With the change in planning fashions there has been a considerable move towards renovating old properties rather than replacing them by new council estates. This happened first in gentrified areas reoccupied by professional families after a gap of over half a century. What was previously regarded as run-of-the-mill Victorian speculative housing suddenly acquired a new status as a fine example of nineteenth-century townscape and domestic architecture, mainly because it was occupied by a barrister and his family rather than half a dozen immigrant families. The fashion spread to areas repurchased by local councils. Many of the conversions were unsuccessful and disliked by the families rehoused in them. Their future life expectancy was less than that of new homes. They do, however, have the advantages of preserving pleasant buildings and familiar surroundings. They can prevent the destruction of a living and long established community. The decision whether to rebuild or renovate is always complex, and usually the only people not to be given a voice in the proceedings are the original residents.

Southwark Council planned to buy the Grosvenor Estate, pull the houses down, rehouse the inhabitants, and create an open space. This information was published in *Compass* with a suggestion that the residents band together in an association to protect their interests. Two months later Douglas Bartles-Smith and Gerry Williams called a meeting of all local residents by announcing it in *Compass*. The meeting took place in St. Michael's Church Hall, the only available local building, and the crowded meeting voted overwhelmingly to form an association and elected twenty-one members to the Committee. Douglas Bartles-Smith and Gerry Williams were invited to all the committee meetings to give informed advice on how to proceed. The committee first undertook a survey to establish what was the course of action preferred by the residents. Over three out of four families living on the estate said that they wished to remain, having their houses restored rather than demolished. Armed with this information the residents' association approached the council and tried to persuade them to refurbish the estate, allowing all residents who so wished to continue to live there. The council agreed. The association then called another meeting for the residents, to which officers of the council and local councillors also came to answer questions. Mr. Barrett the tenants' secretary wrote a report of this meeting and the progress of the association which conveys both his delight at their common achievements and the frustration which so often erupts during consultations with the local council even when there is a large measure of common agreement.

He wrote, 'As secretary of the Grosvenor Estate Residents'

87

Association, I would like to give a purely personal point of view of our recent meeting with the Council. The main point is that the Council has no legal obligation to consult the residents. They could pull the lot down and put up atrocities, they could (as they are going to do) convert the whole lot into self-contained flats, without any consultation. Due to a very strong Residents' Association which pushed for a meeting, and also an obvious moral obligation, the Council did agree to meet us. The thing that gave me and the whole Committee the greatest satisfaction was the tremendous response to our appeal for residents to attend the meeting. In fact there were at least 300 out of a possible 500, which must be some kind of a record! To the Council's credit is the fact that they brought all the people who could answer all of our questions. The only problem was the way they answered them. Members of the Council had already told the Chairman and myself at a preliminary meeting that the Council wanted to keep the estate as near its present condition as they could, and although they would have to move people back and forth, they would keep the inconvenience and cost down to a minimum. This would have been fine if we had not been told two days later at the meeting that we might get as little as three weeks' notice of a move; and also they would not pay the removal costs for residents who want to return to their converted houses. That's what the Council means by keeping costs and inconvenience to a minimum! My last point is that the Council know we have a strong Association and they will respond to pressure – which you can be sure we will exert to its fullest extent.' The association maintained their insistent demands, with the result that the houses on the one-hundred-year-old estate are being converted slowly in a manner which does not disrupt community life.

Few old estates like the Grosvenor have been saved. Much community work is concerned with attempting to nourish the seeds of community on new estates, and to guard their precarious growth. Complaints about the general deficiencies of new estates are rife. Mr. Rogers and his family had lived in ABC Mansions in Bethwin Road and were moved into a new block of flats. He wrote a typical letter to *Compass*. 'ABC, although cheap, was very damp and run-down, and the land-

*i*ord never went out of his way to be helpful, but it was a friendly place to live in, much more friendlier than Hanworth House. We don't know many people here and most of those we do know are people who've moved here from ABC like ourselves. Lots of shortcomings of living in Hanworth House are due to a combination of factors; for example, the Council may fail to clear away the rubbish – and some tenants may continue to send their children with more rubbish, making an ugly, smelly mess.' But Mr. Rogers' main criticisms were reserved for the new system of 'flying squads' of caretakers. 'They seem to do a very superficial job of cleaning the staircases. And the other day the central heating went off. I went to the Assistaphone and reported it; the bloke at the other end said he couldn't possibly pass on the report unless he had another couple of complaints within the half-hour. So I got another couple of people to go and complain. But the heating is still off today. I wonder if they will knock a bit off the rent?' Mr. Rogers discovered that banding together with his neighbours not only speeded rehousing, but was the most effective way of remedying the problems which he found on the new estate. It also helped to cement new friendships, and encouraged the growth of a new community.

The lack of decent cleaning and the slowness in effecting repairs are common complaints on new estates, but an even more serious persistent protest concerns play facilities. Again the words of a local correspondent to *Compass* tell the story vividly and perceptively. Mrs. Rampling recommended action. 'I would like to put forward a suggestion that a play area be made available in Wyndham Road. There are hundreds of children living down and around this road, and there is absolutely nowhere for the children to play. The children in Kevan and Laird House (20-storey tower blocks) especially get into trouble from the porters for making a mess of the square in Kevan House and if they play on the grass by the old people's flats they get told to play elsewhere. I suggest that a piece of wasteland in Wyndham Road be made into a play area with swings etc. and some sort of a football pitch for the children to play in without being moaned at. It is disgusting that the Council has given no forethought to these children when

89

building these high flats.' Mrs. Rampling was not the only local resident who had been worried about the lack of play-space. So great was the agitation that Douglas Bartles-Smith, Gerry Williams, Michael Geater (the chairman of Wyndham Tenants' Association) and the leaders of several other local groups founded a new committee to build a playground in Bethwin Road for the use of local children. This playground committee persuaded the Greater London Council to give them a site and 80% of the necessary money to build a playground. The committee raised another £10,000 and the G.L.C. granted them the other £40,000 and after eight years the playground opened. It includes a football pitch, an adventure area, a corner for small infants and a play building to use when it is wet, cold, or dark.

Castlemead is another new estate, mainly composed of a tall ugly block containing 114 flats. It is situated on a major road junction, but had no play facilities whatever. Its inhabitants were depressed and apathetic. Early in 1968 an extraordinary rumour swept through the block to the effect that the entire building was to be demolished. The council had asked Cambridge House to run a pre-school play group in facilities they were planning to build on the estate. Owing to the council's taciturn reticence, the tenants thought an expanding estate was to be destroyed. Many residents were leaving. Douglas Bartles-Smith and Gerry Williams published an account of the council's future plans in *Compass*. Then they suggested that the formation of a tenants' association could enable residents to be better informed about proposals for their homes.

There are many different ways of starting local groupings of tenants. On the Grosvenor Estate, the local vicar summoned a meeting himself and suggested the idea. Another method is to distribute questionnaires in an area to test reactions to common problems. The keenest residents are then encouraged to call a meeting of all inhabitants to found an association. A third method is to utilize a previously known local resident. In Castlemead this was done through a local Christian teacher, Malcolm Magee. He called together a meeting in his flat of other local Castlemead residents. This small group decided to call a general meeting of all Castlemead tenants which would be combined with an opportunity to meet local councillors and planners who could be questioned in detail about their plans for Castlemead. Malcolm Magee and his fellow residents visited all the other tenants to inform them about the coming discussion while the tedious and infinitely protracted task of persuading the local council to attend such a meeting to consult with the residents began. It took a year to cajole the planners to face the planned. It began in January, 1969 with permission to publish the plans for the estate extension. Later in January the housing manager wrote to say that nothing could be done till the matter had been discussed by the Borough Housing Committee, and until the Ministry had granted loan sanction. When work had actually started on the site a letter was sent to the housing manager stating that it was impossible for tenants to be active participants in future planning unless they were consulted prior to the plans' becoming operational. In February a letter of reply arrived stating that the housing manager had been in touch with the borough architects about the provision of play facilities, and as soon as the information was available a meeting would be profitably held. A month later another letter was sent in an attempt to overcome the delaying tactics of the council officers and which expressed concern over the laggard pace in arranging a meeting. The housing manager replied suggesting a meeting after Easter, but in April and May the borough architects were still discussing a possible display which they claimed would take considerable time to prepare. At the end of May a letter was received claiming that changes were considered necessary to the previous plans, and thus that any meeting would be premature. The residents responded that the best time for a meeting was when plans were being formulated, as this would afford local tenants an ideal opportunity to share in their composition. In June when even this failed to bring a response, Douglas Bartles-Smith had no alternative but to telephone the Architects Department. He discovered that the senior management knew nothing about the proposed meetings, nor about the developments and delays. It finally took place at Castlemead on October 1.

Council representatives divulged that sixty new homes were to be built on the site as well as a Tenants' Hall and a playground area with facilities for a play group. It was decided to

91

form a Castlemead Tenants' Association. The committee was elected that evening. Subsequently this committee entered into an agreement with the borough council for running its own Tenants' Hall and also to organize the play group facilities.

Community work granted those groups who combined together, whether in old slums or on new estates, the opportunity to control wider areas of their lives than was previously possible. They escaped faster from intolerable housing conditions than before. They influenced the modernization of their old homes, the design of their new homes, the provision of play facilities, and improvements in the maintenance and amenities in their new estates. They made themselves a force which could demand and enforce their right to be consulted over matters intimately affecting their future. In achieving these aims they also discovered new friends, new neighbours, new abilities, and the consciousness of new power. Community workers were among the most potent catalysts to promote changes. In time community workers, especially when they are raw newcomers to an area, need to establish useful contacts. In our area the local church has proved most helpful. Not only does it have the premises available for meetings, not only does it have a core of local members in the area, but it also has professional leaders resident in and aware of the immediate situation. Gerry Williams stated, 'I have found clergymen very useful; as they are seen by the locals to be natural members of the community, they often have an intimate knowledge of local problems.' Although the community development approach has been successful, it works best with individual efforts by small groups of workers for voluntary organizations. It is less successful as a part of statutory or governmental services where it can become institutionalized, adopting the errors it was established to combat.

An excellent example of how an inadequately conceived and poorly applied community-work scheme can fail in its stated objectives can be seen in the history of the Community Development Project. On July 16, 1969 the Home Secretary announced in Parliament that community development projects were to be established in Coventry, Glamorgan, Liverpool and Southwark, the last project established in Newington Ward, the northern part of the group ministry area. The Home Secretary stated that it would be 'a neighbourhood-based experiment aimed at finding new ways of meeting the needs of people living in areas of high social deprivation, by bringing together the work of all the social services under the leadership of a special project team, and also by tapping resources of self-help and mutual help which may exist among the people in the neighbourhood.'

The sentiments are impeccable, but the initial actions failed to match up to the words. In December, 1969 local apprehensions were voiced in *Compass*. 'This paper supports any worthwhile community action. But we cannot refrain from asking certain questions at this stage. "How was Newington Ward chosen?" "Why was there no consultation with local people before the choice was made?" These are important questions, for surely the whole point of "Community Work" is to consult the people *before* taking action.'

In January, 1970 Home Office representatives explained the objectives of the Community Development Project to representatives of voluntary organizations in the neighbourhood. The discussion centred on the control of the project. The belief was widely articulated that local people would be excluded from any voice in the project, and that without such representation it would be merely one more example of outside experts, professionals and civil servants making all the vital decisions which affect people's lives without any participation. It was indicated that a local steering committee for the project – composed of local people and representatives from voluntary agencies, local and central-government services – was envisaged. This committee would endeavour 'to secure agreement and support for a programme of action'. Despite being part of the original Home Office plans the committee was never instituted.

It took six months to appoint the project team leader, Florence Rossetti, and she was immediately invited to meet the group ministry council. Through this, and through meetings with the local clergy and church members, considerable pressure was placed on Florence Rossetti to involve local people in the workings of the project.

The project team, however, faced a major difficulty, for one

93

quarter of their income came from the Borough of Southwark who were the joint controlling body. The local councillors, dubious about the project from the first, wished to keep strict financial control over its expenditure. Florence Rossetti had to spend the first six months of her job searching for an office and for a secretary. Lack of finance was a lesser burden to the unenviable position of being thought by the councillors to be heading a revolutionary conspiracy to overturn local government, and by local people to be mere council stooges. This was neatly summed up by a letter from one of the tenants' leaders in the project area. He wrote, 'The idea of local residents on the steering committee has been completely dropped. The council officials now use the C.D.P. headquarters as a regular surgery, not in itself a bad thing but certainly indicative of who is running the show. In fact one local resident at a recent public meeting referred to it as the "committee rooms". The declared aim of the project is that it should be directed by what the local people consider to be *their* needs and that it should translate their needs into action. It cannot do this in the abstract, however willing and determined the members of the project team may be. It must realise that to perpetuate the situation where it does things *for* the local people rather than *with* the local people is to set itself up as just another branch of a system of Local Government.'

This bleak criticism was ignored by the local councillors, and in May, 1972 Florence Rossetti after two years of battling with local councillors and their officers admitted defeat and resigned. She said, 'It's fairly simple. In my view the council have not given the project the necessary support from the beginning. I've given it a good try and I've had enough of frustration.' In an editorial on the resignation *Compass* revealed that an influential group of councillors continually obstructed and opposed the project. The chairman of the Planning Committee actually gave instructions to his staff that the project was not to be given information relating to their work in Newington Ward – this to a project supported and partially financed by the council! The resignation of Florence Rossetti and the subsequent publicity nearly ended the project. It had to advertise three times before it could find a suitable new leader. Some

94

staff lacked previous experience in community work. Much valuable work was done in local schools, playschools and providing advice to local residents but it failed in its prime objective to involve local people in decision-making procedures.

The history of the project also highlights many of the difficulties which beset statutory and governmental agencies in their efforts to transform the inner-city. The social workers involved in the project often privately attempted to press for more community involvement, but they found it impossible to criticize publicly those responsible for their impossible situation.

Both the Seebohm and Skeffington Committees recognized that people must be encouraged to participate in public affairs. But they recommended that community-development workers whose 'role is that of a source of information and expertise, a stimulator, a catalyst and an encourager' should be employed by the local authority. This is a role difficult to reconcile with their other function: to be part of a protest against distant and anonymous authority. A community worker may feel impelled to stimulate a community organization to oppose council policy. When this happens, and it was a constant irritant in the history of the Newington Community Development Project, local politicians will attempt to neutralize the worker – whom they employ to be a tranquillizer, not a stimulant. Any effective community worker must be independent of the local or national government if he is not to be fettered. Where this has not happened the local churches have, as we have emphasized, a unique ability and responsibility to publicize hidden conflicts.

Again and again local clergy and church-members, especially those involved in organizing and running senior citizens' clubs, were regaled with accounts of the failure of the social services to deal adequately with old people's problems, especially after the reorganization of the social services departments. Old people were no longer visited by the social workers who used to call and see them when they were under the care of the old welfare department.

It was agreed by the churches to investigate the situation, and it was soon discovered that the Southwark Social Services Department was near breaking-point. There was a grave shortage of social workers in the area teams, coupled with a high turnover of staff. There had been a rapid increase in the numbers of people who had applied for help, or who had been referred to social workers since the social service department had been reorganized. Owing to this extra pressure the new department was failing to cope adequately with the elderly to whom services had been drastically cut. When this situation was revealed in *Compass* the response was characteristic – an indignant initial denial by the Director of Southwark Social Services Department that the problem existed, followed in a matter of weeks by his appeal to voluntary organizations to care for old people in situations that had been handled by the old welfare department. Until the churches uncovered and publicized the deplorable services for old people, the problem did not officially exist. The old people were not being visited, yet nobody had thought of asking for help from the local community. Eighteen months later, after further publicity, the Director of the Social Services met the editor of *Compass*. The only solution suggested by senior social workers was a large increase in the numbers of social workers employed. There was no recognition that an alternative strategy was practical, whereby social workers might be redeployed to urgent priorities and encourage local people to meet the less urgent needs.

Another problem which was highlighted by the church was the growing disillusionment of local residents with the professional workers in the area. The members of the churches continually indicated that because social workers, teachers, doctors, housing officials and planners did not reside in North Southwark they could not really grasp what life there was like, what were the most pressing problems and what solutions stood the best chance of success. Their knowledge of the area was second-hand, derived from meeting their clients in offices, their patients in surgeries, their pupils in schools. The majority of adequate adults never met any local teachers or planners or social workers. The problem was easy to identify yet difficult to solve. A start was made with a series of citizens' forums when one subject – education, health, housing or the social services – would be examined, and local residents and professionals locally concerned with the subject could compare views and eradicate misconceptions about the topic involved.

This was yet another way in which independent groups of people, whether churches, settlements or others working in the inner-city were able to work towards a robust community life. Improved conditions, better housing, more choice, more participation and more power are goals which have too often been opposed by the local councillors, planners and social workers who are best able to facilitate them. All too easily they have tried to create achievements by shortcuts, by consulting only 'expert' opinions, by concentrating power in their own hands. All too often local residents have remained apathetic and defeated, resigned to the belief that nothing can be changed. Churches and other groups who are independent of the power structures will be increasingly needed to mediate, to reconcile, challenge, prompt and encourage in the urban ghetto. In the five years the group ministry has been established the number of self-help groups in the area has swollen from two to well over a dozen.

Many of these groups have relied on the help of settlements and churches to provide them with expert help, with premises to meet, simple facilities for administrative chores and a medium for publicity. For both settlements and churches have always seen their work as having both individual and corporate significance. Settlements were placed in poor but established communities. Churches have always been placed at the centre of community life, whether in a country village or an urban slum. Their strength or weakness has largely reflected the vigour of its surrounding community. In the inner-city all community life has declined. Political parties, attendances at football matches and organized sports – all have declined. Churches have closed, but in far fewer numbers than pubs and cinemas. Unless community life can be revived there is little hope for radically transforming the environment which constitutes the urban ghetto of today. The community-development approach can help not just to found tenants' groups, but also to revive life in many declining institutions. It may be one way to enable the churches and other institutions not just to survive, but to flourish. It can also be of use to the clergy. They can see and criticize the weaknesses of others working in the inner-city and take new initiatives. They can also have their own efforts

97

examined to see whether they and their churches are helping to rebuild or to demolish a vigorous community life.

The urban crisis is far too serious and its causes far too desperate to be solved by a more detailed application of the community-development approach or by a large increase in community workers employed by voluntary agencies. It would be a mistake to imagine that a community approach has been uniformly successful. There have been occasions when local groups of people have been offered the chance to form tenants' or residents' associations and have rejected the proposals.

As well as areas with no community organizations, there has been a misuse of community work. Sometimes local residents were left to cope with situations for which they had as yet neither the technical knowledge nor the experience. In one example in Warrior Road the tenants' representatives came away from a meeting convinced that all the houses were to be demolished when in fact the authorities had guaranteed to destroy only two out of every three homes. If there had been a community worker at the meeting it is probable that those people living in old slums would have been rehoused earlier.

Although tenants' associations can do much, there are limits to their powers. Some are formed with the sole purpose of helping their members to escape from intolerable conditions in dripping tenements. Others, like most inner-city institutions, are run by the usual handful of dedicated people, while the other tenants are prepared to sit back apathetically and do nothing but moan. The Annual General Meeting of a tenants' group will often number only twenty or thirty people and they will elect the committee which will represent the whole estate. Some committees will concentrate almost all the energies on running socials, dances, Bingo and outings rather than really take up tenants' grievances with authorities. Some tenants' associations will not themselves really represent natural community areas and groupings. No tenants' association has succeeded in organizing visits for old people. This has contrasted with the much better support for schemes involving the running of youth activities.

The community development approach is no magic panacea which can solve every urban problem. It is, however, one of the few signs of hope in a desperate and deteriorating situation, one of the few attempts which have shown promise not only of solving several of the appalling physical problems which beset the inner-city, but also of combating and even overcoming the manifest apathy and fatalism. Local tenants' associations have survived. This is a great initial achievement. They should be able to achieve more as the years advance. Yet the pace of change is dispiritingly slow; limits are seen to what self-help can achieve. Gerry Williams wrote recently, 'The story has been one of disappointment and frustration. Firstly, local groups can only hope to achieve their aims if the local government structure is receptive to their views and prepared to accept the principle of consultation. But the concept of participation/consultation is still a new one and the local authorities' reaction has been guarded and slow. It cannot be stated strongly enough that if local people are to be encouraged to participate in group activity aimed at improving the quality of life in their neighbour-hood, then this activity can only be fulfilling if their contribution is appreciated and seen to be of value, and if they have some chance of achieving what they are fighting for. Too often committed people's backs are broken by the amount of work they have to undertake in the very limited time at their disposal, and the victories they achieve for this work are often too rare to make the commitment worthwhile.'

Another serious weakness in the field of community work has been in the type of people who are helped by the approach. The very inadequate families and individuals are only rarely involved or helped by community workers. The tenants' committees tend to be drawn from among the more capable, articulate and aspiring members of the community. Workers in the community field have found it easier to develop such people, to further their skills, to teach them the best way to discover the appropriate functionaries. They learn quickly the most effective letters to write to officials, how to overcome delaying tactics, and the most appropriate methods of leadership so that groups do not become over-dependent on their community adviser.

It is easier to be pessimistic than euphoric in the inner-city, but the community development approach can play a large part in solving the outstanding problems. All professional workers in the inner-city should in their training be given adequate guidance into the community element in their work, whether they are priests, teachers, doctors, planners or youth workers. Just as important, anyone concerned by the plight of the cities must understand that unless the voices of the dispossessed are heard there can be no solution to urban problems. Everyone must work to build up human communities where they live, to allow people the opportunity to state their own needs and by co-operative endeavours to solve them. Community work is an effort to convince the poor that they can control their destiny and that they do have a future.

8. The Destruction of the Ghetto

Inner-city areas have declined as the suburbs have increased. But they still contain millions of people, and encapsulate the problems of poverty, crime, unemployment, slums and human despair which both threaten and judge our society. We have described one typical inner-city neighbourhood, its historic growth, and the causes of its many problems. We have indicated the advantages which voluntary agencies possess as catalysts for renewal, and the disadvantages under which statutory bodies labour. We have described a few of the small triumphs in working to improve our area. We have shown that residents' groups, churches, parents' associations and other local groups must be the focus for action in the inner-city.

Not all the problems of the inner-city, however, can be solved from within its boundaries. The inner-city is an isolated area in our society. Inside a ghetto its community can ameliorate their own hardships, and give people a strong sense of identity and purpose, but its inhabitants cannot destroy the walls of the ghetto that imprison them. They need outside help. An analysis of urban deprivation published in December, 1975 by the Central Statistical Office confirms that the inner-city areas remain the most underprivileged parts of the nation. They have the worst housing, lacking many basic amenities, high unemployment, and low incomes. The report states, 'It was found that census enumeration districts with extensive levels of deprivation generally occur within the conurbations, and that local authorities making up the central cores of the conurbations contain proportionately more of them than the rest of the conurbation.' The inner-city areas in Clydeside and London, Merseyside and Birmingham are areas in desperate need of regeneration. Until they are cured the whole of society will remain sick. Little time remains. The spectre of American inner-city areas reminds us that there are depths of alienation, crime, brutality, drugs and racial strife that we have not begun to plumb.

Central districts of cities become repositories for the losers of society, with the able leaders fleeing to the suburbs. Vandalism and crime increase. Respect for the law and the police decrease. A 1975 police report on Kirby in Liverpool said many inhabitants accepted criminal activities as normal. Crimes were committed openly without fear of intervention by onlookers who were frightened of reprisals. Vandalism cost the area £400,000 in 1974. Most shops had bricked-up windows. Seven hundred flats had been totally vandalized and it would cost £4,000,000 to renovate them. Assaults on the police are common. Crimes by juveniles increase with great rapidity.

Much of the crime and vandalism stems from problem families who cause social stress disproportionate to their numbers. The parents in such families lack the ability and stamina needed to rear children satisfactorily in difficult conditions. Such families cannot base their self-respect upon income or possessions or skills. They are almost immune to social pressures and public opinion. They are isolated, and contract out of normal community life. Such families whose destructive abilities are out of all proportion to their numbers are concentrated in the urban ghettos. As more mobile families leave, the problem families form a higher percentage of the total households. As the numbers in the inner-city decline, the problems and the deprivation intensify. Those receiving governmental relief rise. People withdraw from community problems into private concerns. Ethnic hostility grows as groups fight to gain an increased share of scarce resources. The walls of the ghetto become higher and wider. It is in the eventual interests of all suburban residents as well as the urban poor, to prevent this happening.

It is not easy to see a clear scenario for constructive change in the inner-city. Our society is so structured that the poverty of the central areas contributes to the wealth, health and contentment of many others in affluent exurbia. The urban poor are seen as a peril to be rejected rather than as people to be helped. The existence of two separate but overlapping cultures ignorant of each other prevents progress. Radical change can only result from the will of the majority of the people. Yet only a declining minority of the inhabitants of industrial countries live in the inner-city. They are people with little economic strength, a muted voice, and small influence on the levers of power. They are often leaderless, apathetic and disillusioned. Yet to solve their problems they need substantial outside help which has been consistently denied them. In a chill economic climate it is difficult to enlist the resources which they desperately need.

There are some hopeful signs that changes may be possible. There are many groups, churches, political organizations, educationalists and unions that are attempting to remedy the injustices of the inner-city. Consultation and participation are established as dogmas to which local authorities and planners pay reverent homage. Their effectiveness depends on the degree and speed of consultation, but at least the old system of the uncaring deciding for the unknowing has declined.

There is a growing realization, first by the Liberals and Communists and then by other parties, that community politics is a considerable force. Political parties have assumed the continual loyalty of their private soldiers while the generals were plotting global and national strategies. Some of the political privates have committed mutiny, in Newham and elsewhere, and they will need to be offered more local control if they are to serve again. Although it would be unwise to expect too much from the belated recognition by national politicians of the political importance of local action, there are signs throughout the world that there is real power growing in neighbourhood politics.

The last hopeful omen for change is the growth of knowledge about the inner-city. Analysis must precede action. The greater the knowledge, the greater the likelihood that the urban ghetto can be transformed. There has been sufficient historical research into the origins of urban poverty, enough sociological research into urban community deprivation, an abundance of economic research into the absence of resources, and a plethora of psychological research into the causes of apathy, despair and breakdown among the urban poor. Ignorance about the nature and extent of the problems of the inner-city has declined. A

103

conference in 1975 called for the urgent regeneration of London's East End. Peter Walker, the former Environment Secretary warned, 'The problems of our major conurbations are deteriorating at a very fast rate. There will be considerable increase in racial friction in our bigger cities if the present trends of high unemployment, collapse of education and increasing truancy, and deterioration of housing continue.' Knowledge should lead to action although it is easy to explain away uncomfortable facts, to postpone unpalatable decisions and to plead the need for more research.

Radical change will only occur when all these hopeful developments coincide. It may not arrive until the situation deteriorates still further with a resultant surge of local action and an explosive eruption by distressed and persecuted minorities in the inner-city. Despite the traditional stability and restraint of the urban poor they include amongst their number many social deviants who could become dominant if the situation continues to degenerate. All institutions, whether churches, settlements, schools or local councils risk being further identified with the oppressors of the inner-city poor unless they detach themselves from the reactionary political and social stance and the cultural myopia which have often characterized them in the past. They have often (consciously or not) helped to perpetuate a system which was grossly prejudicial to the urban poor.

Change cannot be imposed from above, and the history of the last quarter of a century makes one sceptical of the ability of the statutory agencies to initiate change however great the resources of money, assets and personnel that they are granted. These agencies have alienated local communities, failed to identify problems, and have proved unable to stimulate local initiatives. Living in poverty has its own destructive effect on human capacities, and these impairments perpetuate deprivation. Both the internal disabilities of the poor and the external factors that breed them must be tackled simultaneously or failure is certain. The statutory agencies have failed to do this. The time has come to channel more resources to the voluntary agencies which are smaller and closer to those they help. They are more successful in engaging volunteers, more flexible to changing needs, and far more economical in terms of money and manpower. They are far better at co-operating with local individuals and groups. The statutory agencies are imprisoned by their bureaucratic apparatus, by their monolithic structures and by the impossibility of effectively criticizing their political masters. They are enormously expensive. London local councils alone in 1974 were in debt to the tune of four thousand million pounds. The numbers of employees and the financial costs of local government have risen far more than any other section of national life, yet services have declined. In our Borough of Southwark one of every twenty workers is employed by the local council. In the social services department alone there are over 2,500 employees of whom only 123 are area social workers. Despite huge numbers of employees and vast expenditures the statutory agencies have been slow to identify and meet the needs of groups varying from the single homeless to adult illiterates. They are cumbersome and grossly wasteful bodies with few effective criteria for assessing the success or failure of their activities. They seem unable to admit failure, or to reverse unsuccessful policy decisions.

All the programmes to help the inner-city have failed because none of them has enabled the poor to act on behalf of their own interests. The current social work solution to urban problems is modern colonialism, working with indigenous leaders only when they act the role of obedient tribal chiefs. Education is compensatory, offering as a substitute for integration a training for all the dirty jobs left over in automated industries. The ghetto is repaired, not demolished. The poor are offered no share of the power, wealth, privilege or knowledge of the powerful. New social, economic and political resources must be granted to the poor so that they will have the power to reduce significantly their own inequality. All outside help has failed because of the fierce resistance at national and municipal level to allowing the poor themselves to be given the chance to determine their own priorities. Any other approach reinforces the dependency and perpetuates the powerlessness of the poor.

There needs to be a co-ordinated attack on the problem by all the groups and organizations involved in the inner-city. This must be aimed at positively favouring the victims of deprivation in employment, education and housing. There must be a

105

concerted endeavour to establish a flexible approach to social planning, to organize what is organic, to build a new extended family and a strong community. There must be not only the central government research that emanates from the Urban Deprivation Unit but also a listening to what the deprived think and say are their problems and needs. As Samuel Johnson wrote of those who ruled the highlands of Scotland,

> They are strangers to the language, and the manners, to the advantages and wants of the people, whose life they would model, and whose evils they would remedy.

That is also true today of those who decide about the needs of the poor in the inner-city.

Radical change cannot occur without an idea of what is wrong in the present situation coupled with a clear perspective about what must be altered. The greatest impetus for change is a clear consensus about which elements take priority in the united attack on the problem.

Housing remains the first priority. It is grossly over-optimistic to assume that the old slums will vanish into renovated or rebuilt homes, but even if this were true the problem is no longer one of providing all homes with a bathroom, toilet, kitchen and hot and cold running water. No one can walk round our area of North Southwark without realizing that some of the century-old properties are well liked and well cared for by a settled and homogeneous community despite their lacking certain amenities. The converse of this situation is that in the same area there are three year-old blocks of council housing that are dirty, disreputable and badly vandalized. It cost £500,000,000 in 1974 to maintain public housing, much of it repairing vandals' damage. The occupants of such housing are often ashamed to ask their friends to visit them. Rebuilding and replanning is far more than the provision of basic, minimal amenities.

There is a great need for a more diverse social mix in the inner-city. A ghetto is formed when separate groups of people are herded together. They cannot leave. Others cannot enter. The ghetto intensifies. This has been the history of most inner-city areas. There is a desperate need for a more varied mixture of professions and of accommodation, particularly for middle income owner-occupiers. This demand cannot be the responsibility of the local councils burdened by a long housing list of people in desperate surroundings, and with a very small amount of available land for rebuilding. Suburban councils must release more land for the urban poor to move to municipal housing in the outer suburbs. In exchange more owner-occupiers must be given a financial stimulus to move to the inner-city areas.

Another grave injustice is that much of the housing in the cities is under-occupied. A husband and wife with four children can never compete on the open housing market with a single man or a working couple with no children at home. So we have the ludicrous situation that a family with several children are often crammed into a small flat that would be perfectly suitable for the childless couple who, by virtue of their combined earnings, may well be living in the four-bedroomed house that the larger family needs and desires. Housing for families with dependent children should, therefore, be subsidized at the expense of households without dependent children. This must be applied rigorously to under-occupied municipal housing, and even more importantly, to the large amounts of empty or under-occupied houses which are privately owned. It is impossible to increase the total housing stock in cities except very slowly. But houses can be distributed better to eliminate shortages. It would also help if individuals or companies were not allowed to keep homes in the central areas of cities in addition to owning properties elsewhere. It is grossly unjust that some families should own two homes while others are desperately short of adequate accommodation.

Unless people feel a sense of responsibility for their own homes and environment, vandalism and neglect will continue. Local councils should swallow their ideological objections to private ownership, and attempt to find reasonable schemes by which council tenants can be given a financial stake in their own homes, and corporately manage their own estates. We have a situation where, due to rapid inflation, a council tenant may well have paid more in rent for his home after forty years' tenancy than he would have had to pay if he could have taken out a mortgage on the same house. Yet he has received no tax relief on his rent as he would have had on a mortgage, nor has he any financial rights in his home at the end of his tenancy. Recent plans by the Greater London Council and Birmingham Council to enable tenants to pay a mortgage and not a rent for at least half of their homes should be encouraged and extended. No more vast, new estates with their enormous maintenance costs should be erected. Instead, cheap terraced housing must be built for sale to inner-city residents, especially the newly-married skilled workers. More houses and fewer flats must be the pattern for the future, and by eliminating the useless, grassed areas that surround blocks of flats, the new terraced houses can be given small, individual yards and gardens.

As well as making more private properties available in inner-city areas there need to be widespread endeavours to persuade more middle-class people to live in inner-city areas. This would improve their understanding, provide much needed skills and leadership in the inner-city, and help to raise the standards in schools, societies and general amenities. Many of the most able professional workers opt for an easier life in the suburbs. They need financial incentives to encourage them to live and work in needy inner-city areas just as industries receive grants to site factories in development areas. Special housing grants should be given to make it more practical for them to reside in the area. Housing could be specifically built for teachers, youth workers and social workers as it has been for firemen and policemen. Work in schools and youth clubs in the inner-city is more difficult than in the suburbs. There needs to be a much better teacher-pupil ratio in the inner-city than elsewhere. Teachers and youth service workers need to be better paid in the central areas of the cities than they are on the peripheries. This should eventually raise the school standards in the inner-city, reduce crime and vandalism and thus ultimately recoup any additional expenditure.

It is not to be expected that the gross discrepancies between schools will alter immediately. At present only 12% of boys at comprehensive schools enter higher education, with the over-whelming number of these coming from comprehensives sited in middle-class areas. Yet 66% of girls from direct-grant girls' schools enter higher education. With society allocating jobs that are powerful, interesting, and remunerative on the basis of educational qualifications, able children from the inner-city ghettos of the urban poor will be denied a reasonable share of these jobs. A large percentage of the places in institutes of higher education should be awarded on a basis of area quotas rather than on the present national basis of academic competitions in which the scales are weighted in favour of the suburban child. However, in order that the urban children who qualify for such higher education are not hopelessly handicapped the education of the urban child should be far more intensive than it is at present. Parents should be informed that unless their children work hard and learn steadily they will be condemned to be the drudges of society in the future as they have been in the past. Education must be designed to broaden the experience of children not merely to fit them for acquiescent life inside the ghetto walls. Education will emphasize attainment and achievement. Rewards and punishments will be cheerfully embraced as stimuli to the inevitably competitive nature of children, and not guiltily shunned as unegalitarian. Discipline will have to be based on the realization that destructive children must be controlled and curbed unless the work of all is to be irredeemably disturbed. As more and more teachers move to live in the inner-city they will base their teaching on reality, not fantasy.

In education as in other areas of local government, more resources and not less should be given to voluntary and church schools. Only in these schools has there been effective local and parental control. State schools are controlled by teachers and by the school inspectorate. When parents were begging for small, varied schools, they were building huge, uniform, neighbourhood comprehensive schools that offered no real educational choice to parents. The recent clamour for educational vouchers has sprung from the realization that the poor have no educational choices open to them.

Nobody is more despised by the urban poor than the idle sponger. The poor are too close to the option of social security not to resent those who choose it without a compelling reason. Yet many receive some statutory help in the form of supplementary pensions, or unemployment benefits, or rent rebates, or free school meals. Their number grows annually, and in

Inner London they comprise half the inhabitants. This saps confidence and self-reliance. More should be done by reforming welfare allowances to encourage work as a solution to poverty, and not to encourage extra welfare provisions.

The inner-city desperately needs work for its residents. Unemployment is far higher here than elsewhere. Over a third of the manufacturing jobs in Inner London have been lost in the last fifteen years. Some jobs must come from large developments, from encouraging new transport links and factory building. But more could be done at a much smaller level. Small warehouses, yards and shops have been ruthlessly swept away by wholesale redevelopment, while the endless planning regulations and complicated legal constraints prevent the development of small, local industries and trades to replace those lost. The inner-city is a repository of great skills, initiative and commercial sense. But the opportunities to create new jobs are denied by total planning. Local industries are destroyed, pride is harmed and many jobs are lost. The greatest practical needs in the inner-city are for good housing and decently paid employment. The vast bulk of the money spent in the inner-city must be channelled in this direction, and away from the money spent on salaries for those who try to patch up the problems caused by unemployment and poor housing.

Jobs have a social value in the community as well as a monetary value in the market place. A month without hospital workers, dustmen, or transport workers results in appalling social consequences. There must be public recognition, coupled with a narrowing of wage differentials, that the worth of a man or woman cannot be measured by the size of their incomes. The urban poor are worse paid, worse educated, and worse housed than the middle classes. Their jobs are usually regarded as simple, unimportant and overpaid. The lack of social esteem is immense. The Chinese and Cuban experiments to make teachers work on farms, peasants teach in schools, and soldiers build dams has much to recommend it. Any wide interchange of jobs would help to destroy contempt and condescension, and help to establish greater social unity.

The establishment of local councils for each small neighbourhood could bring local representatives back to individual streets. Such councils could be given rights of decision over exclusively local matters, and a veto over matters which concerned their particular neighbourhood. They could be used to ascertain the temperature of public opinion about plans proposed by the borough councils. They could disseminate information to their individual members and convey grassroots feelings to wider bodies. Their main function would be to act as public watchdogs barking angrily when abuses were discovered. Their role would not be to add one more rung to an endless local government ladder, but to reduce large, centralized, local government staff numbers.

One of the great casualties of local government reform is lack of involvement. The more extensive the local government area the more remote it becomes from its constituents, and local government is no longer local. It is remote government. The larger the area the lower the number of voters. There is something uninspiring about local government elections when a 25% turnout is considered reasonable and 50% excellent. Elections need to be more frequent than once every four years. Professional workers must be made more responsible to local residents whose lives are affected by their decisions. It is ironical that while local councillors are theoretically responsible to the electorate, the council officials who often make many of the actual decisions are neither directly involved with nor responsible to electors.

The inner-city environment is inferior to the suburbs'. It is noisier. The traffic is heavier. There is more industrial pollution. It is more crowded with far higher population densities, and with a far lower percentage of gardens. The housing is more crowded; consequently more amenities are needed, yet facilities are woefully inadequate. There is a pitiful lack of parks, woods, open space, gardens, allotments and playgrounds. In a heavily built-up area it is difficult and costly to provide open space, but it is an urgent necessity. The open space must be planned in far more versatile a manner than as the standard patch of grass surrounded by roaring lorries, flanked by ugly blocks of flats and interspersed by sad trees. Play areas must be designed so that children can use them as they wish. They must be insulated from local residents' homes. There should be more well staffed

111

and well structured playgrounds to stimulate and encourage the children.

Local authorities can be improved in many ways. They could use local volunteers and local paid workers instead of expensive professional outsiders. These could visit old people, help teachers in classrooms, liaise with local council officials and serve in other useful capacities. This cannot happen until professional workers learn to share and not hoard their expertise. A reformed body of statutory workers will succeed only if they are committed to the inner-city, and if they encourage participation. Yet even with these reforms it is obvious that local government acts like a dinosaur, with its vast bulk, slow and unwieldy movements, and tiny brain. The economic crisis allows us to examine it dispassionately. More teachers and greater costs have not meant better schools and improved education. More social workers have not meant fewer broken families, less mental illness, and better care for the old. More architects have not meant improved housing. More planners have meant broken, not united communities. And for all the professional workers there has grown an army of clerks, telephonists, press officers, typists, caretakers, cleaners, administrators, technicians and co-ordinators. The waste and profligacy are appalling. The time has come to carve much of it away. It is money ill spent, a waste of human resources. It destroys individual and community responsibility. The functions between different tiers of local government must be clarified so that the interminable delays can be reduced. There is a need for permissive legislation which can be activated by the efforts of those involved in local areas through their homes or their labours. Voluntary societies, churches, settlements, local groups could all be given financial aid and resources in response to their proven ability to generate improvements.

Widespread changes need to be made if the inner-city areas are not to remain festering sores inflaming and polluting our whole society. The growing resentment and antagonism of inner-city residents ensures that no partial ameliorations or minor reforms will purchase their acquiescence. Tragedy can only be averted if all the reforms, of land use, housing, education, local government, social mobility, employment, and economic opportunity begin at once. There must be a massive shift in resources from the suburbs to the inner-city. The poor must be enabled to change their environment, to control the available resources. They must be regarded as partners and not supplicants. Even a small but significant improvement in their level of life and hope would liberate unsuspected strengths. Rising hopes lead to creative actions.

The disastrous consequences of our present position can only be averted by a real concern for the needs and aspirations of all segments of society. The ultimate interests of both workers and managers converge, not diverge. Yet the problems of society will not be solved by appeals to self-interest, nor by the gradual growth of enlightened, liberal and progressive opinions. Whether in housing, employment or education, liberal solutions are usually ineffective. Problem families, however well housed, remain troublesome and often cause the rapid degeneration of their new estate. The minority of idlers cannot be tempted back to work by easy and profitable employment. School rebels react against progressive education in modern schools by truancy or disruption just as vigorously as they did against rote learning in Victorian buildings. Discipline and responsibility are needed at home, work, school, and during leisure pursuits. Malefactors and sluggards have never reformed anything.

In order to eliminate poverty in our urban ghettos we need a crusade for human hope and human dignity for those who have been denied them. Many despair of change. Many lack hope. Unless people from all areas and all professions and all interests combine together in a new vision of the future, there are no prospects for any radical changes to our society. The church which has such a vision must form one group campaigning for change. It has the advantage of working both in the urban ghettos and throughout the nation. It works with all people of all classes. It should comfort the afflicted and afflict the comfortable. Historically, religion has often been a conservative influence, a stabilizing force. It has provided society with a comprehensive scheme of meaning, a universal framework within which particular social institutions, convictions, values and practices find their significance, and which gives them their ultimate justification. Religion overarches society as a sacred canopy. The church must withdraw its sanctification of our society with its destructive differentiation between the overfed and the undernourished, the rich and the poor. Our society provides little individual fulfilment and few balanced communities. The church must work to build a better society, based on creative intelligence, designed to increase the quality of living for all its members. The church must work to influence the political and moral attitudes and behaviour of its members to redress intolerable wrongs. The church must shape and share its vision of the future with teachers and journalists, politicians and planners, community leaders and unionists, with all groups and individuals who care about justice. It must do this as a national institution working with other national bodies and, more importantly, on a local parochial level.

The church is one of the few bodies working in the inner-city which has not been overcome by disillusionment and despair at the enormity of the problems. This is not only due to its own inherently optimistic vision and faith, but also because it is – and by its very nature must be – rooted in the locality.

Radical change can only occur in the inner-city if it is precipitated by a united effort from inside and outside the ghetto. The inner-city must be treated as a priority area. Yet in an economic crisis its financial resources are being drastically reduced just when its problems demand special treatment. Any extra resources are bound at this time to be meagre, and it is thus essential that the money is wisely spent. The finances must not be squandered, as in the past, on yet more salaries for professional workers. It must be used to provide more jobs, better housing and other direct benefits to the local individuals and groups in the inner-city. Directing resources from the suburbs to the tenements will eliminate a potent cause of hatred and social strife, but even such a beneficial change can only occur if all the people who know and care about the problem strive together to achieve it.

The inner-city environment will never be transformed by mere government initiatives, nor by the sole efforts of its inhabitants, however heroic they may be. It is a problem so vast, with so many causes, such a complex web of deprivation, such a history of failure, that it can never be solved by politicians,

114

social workers, teachers or clergy, all acting on their own. The problem can be solved only by united action, and only if the conscience of the nation is aroused to the plight, the desperate plight and gross deprivation of millions of its most powerless members.

At heart, the inner-city is about the indomitable resilience and humour of its people. These are the ones who have survived all its gross disadvantages. They have built living communities in impossible circumstances. In our area, as in many others, the numerous tenants' associations, playground committees and other self-help groups mentioned in the last chapter continue to flourish. Tenants' leaders fight the council for play facilities for their members' children, and for halls to build up a sense of community. Church groups care for their members, maintain their buildings and work in the community. Ninety-year-old ladies invite the local children to their birthday parties. Mothers band together to found playgroups. Fathers run football teams for their sons. It is by giving such united groups support, encouragement and power that the situation can be changed. The inner-city should not be a replica of the outer suburbs, but a place where its people are given the housing, jobs, education and opportunities they desire; and a greater willingness to build on the efforts of its residents could destroy the savage inequities which mock hope and opportunity and freedom for those millions of our fellow human beings who exist in the urban ghetto.